LOOKING UP

LIVING IN ANTICIPATION OF CHRIST

LOOKING UP
LIVING IN ANTICIPATION OF CHRIST

BY
EDDIE TURNER

selective image
BOOKS

Copyright © 2018 by Eddie Turner

ISBN 978-1-7321714-0-4

Selections of Scripture used in this book are borrowed from the KJV, NIV, NASB and ESV translations of the Holy Bible.

More information about books by Eddie Turner can be found at selectiveimage.net/books.

All rights reserved. No part of this book may be reproduced in any form without the written permission of the author except in the case of brief quotations for the purposes of reviewing or promoting.

For my pastors, Bill, James, and Jimmy.

Your love, guidance, and friendship are
the hidden treasures in my field.

CONTENTS

1 Two Words   1

2 A Heated Discussion   7

3 American Idols   13

4 Path of Least Resistance   19

5 Unspoken Word   25

6 Required Reading   31

7 Mission Accomplished?   37

8 Holy Communication   45

9 Good Mythical Marriage   51

10 A Prideful People   59

11	Out of This World	65
12	Credible Witness	71
13	A Testimony	83
14	Excessive Perfection	89
15	First Love	95
16	Sin & Treatment	103
17	Know Your Enemy	109
18	Predictive Text	115
19	Signs & Signals	121
20	Found Worthy	133

1 Two Words

Can you recall two words that absolutely changed your life? I'd pause while you think on this for a bit, but taking a break right off the bat can't be a good thing for an author. Maybe later. My guess is that you're thinking of something along the lines of, "I'm pregnant" or "I do." These are great choices that spark some wonderful memories. These words, however, have just as much potential to incite negative reactions. How they are perceived depends on the context surrounding the use of these words.

Take, for example, the words, "You won." Hearing these words may have caused you to jump for joy if you were the tenth caller on a radio show. Hearing these same words delivered to the tenth caller after you were named the ninth might have made you want to throw your phone in frustration. So, it's easy to see how two words can send those who hear them down opposite paths. Now, suppose the two words in question were in the form of an instruction or a command. Our choice to either react in obedience or to disregard the words altogether would be dependent upon two contextual factors—what you're being told to do and the intention of the person who's telling you to do it. Let's say you were given the instruction, "Be quiet." If a librarian told you this because you were disturbing people who are trying to study, the instruction would be reasonable and worthy of obeying. Given by someone with an opposing view who rudely interrupted your turn to speak, this instruction might warrant a two-word command of your own. You might even give your turn a little more volume.

From these examples, I think we can all understand how reactions to instruction vary greatly. Surprising as it may seem, these same varied reactions occur among church-going men and women in response to the many instructions found in the Bible. In these instances, we are commanded to perform and refrain from acting out various human behaviors. Each command is guaranteed to be in our best interest to follow, yet we tend to pick and choose over the ones we feel are worth obeying. At the same time, we dare not discredit the command giver—the God of this world whose will for our lives is perfect. I don't know about you. But, to me, this creates an enormous conflict.

Before we go any further, I feel that I must address the validity of this book we call our Bible. In it, God gives us the assurance that all Scripture comes from Him and is profitable for our lives. Because Scripture is defined as the whole text that appears within its pages, we must recognize the Bible in its entirety as being completely free of falsehood and unprofitable instruction. If you believe that the Bible contains inconsistencies that were introduced by man, you must consider whether God would allow the instrument He designed to draw His children to Him to become ineffective at doing so. If this were to occur, wouldn't God's command for us to trust in Him become untrustworthy? I'm certain it would. Thankfully, the Bible is now what it has always been—God's perfect instruction for all who live and breathe on this earth.

Now, let's begin together by examining one of the many instructions given by our Savior, Jesus Christ. In it, we will be focusing on two words that may change your life. Those words are *look* and *up*.

Now when these things begin to happen, look up and lift up your heads, because your redemption draws near.

Luke 21:28

In our world, there are two kinds of people who call themselves Christians. What separates these two groups is the attitude each has toward Christ. Which group one belongs to, however, is not something you can detect right away. While following people around and examining their day-to-day activities will give you a good idea of which side of the fence they are on, you can take a much easier and less creepy approach by just striking up a conversation.

On the surface, there are many similarities these two groups share. Both have at least some knowledge of the Bible, both go to church, and both claim to love Jesus. But only one group's members are truly *looking* for him. Because this "looking" is often taken out of context, my goal for this entire book is to put it back in. But first, let's take a closer look the word, *up*. We all know this word refers to the direction that is opposite of down. Simple, right? I mean, Jesus went upward when he departed from the earth, didn't he? He certainly did as Scripture tells us. And we know, also from Scripture, that he will be coming back down.

So, "look up" must simply be an instruction to keep our eyes toward the clouds, right? Not at all. Just think of all the neck pain we'd endure if it was. Christians are not expected to see the returning

Christ from an earthly position. Why? It's because we won't be on the earth. Rather, we will be alongside Jesus when he returns, having been raised from earth to heaven years beforehand. Many people call this event "the rapture." I call it our big exit. It is those who miss the exit that may actually experience some neck pain when Jesus makes his triumphant return.

So, who is supposed to be looking up? Everyone. I see some of you scratching your heads. I hope you held your place in the book with your other hand. If you didn't, don't worry. I'm guessing we're only on page 5. Maybe 6. I know there's a number down there, but I won't see it until later. Hopefully, we're all on the same page as we continue to explore in greater detail how we can obey Jesus' command to look up. Upon doing so, it is my prayer that you may find yourself in full obedience to another of Jesus' two-word commands. "Follow me."

2 A Heated Discussion

In the first chapter, I presented a contrast between Christian attitudes. Jesus also did this by describing one's usefulness in terms of temperature. If you've ever applied a compress to an aching muscle, you know that its soothing power is dependent upon it being hot or cold. There's just no benefit to using one otherwise as Jesus demonstrates here.

I know your deeds, that you are neither cold nor hot; I wish that you were cold or hot. So because you are lukewarm, and neither hot nor cold, I will spit you out of my mouth.

Revelation 3:15-16

Jesus included this message while dictating one of seven letters that the Apostle John transcribed. John was approaching his golden years when Jesus paid him this visit. It's an amazing encounter you can read about at the beginning of the book of Revelation.

These letters served as performance evaluations of the seven most influential churches in Asia Minor (modern-day Turkey). Jesus offered both praise and disapproval according to where each one registered on his special thermometer. And it was the church at Philadelphia that got hit with the lukewarm warning; a warning that should be heeded by both churches and individuals throughout the world today. While a room-temperature compress might have been a good choice as an example, I've never reacted to one with the disgust that Jesus obviously has for the lukewarm. So, let's go with coffee.

Imagine visiting your local Starbucks and ordering your favorite coffee. This is a tough one, I know. Yes, I know some of you are there now. Humor me. So, when you order your flavor of choice that you've enjoyed on numerous occasions, you have the expectation that it will be made the same way it was during each of your previous visits. This time, however, you are caught off guard when the coffee prepared for you was not properly heated. It wasn't cold, but room temperature; the way residents in 49 of our 50 states will NOT take their coffee. Florida is the weird one if you must know.

Now your first sip makes you cringe. This is something you would never willingly put in your mouth. And, now that it's in there, your body wants it out. So, without even a second's time to forge a strategy, the patron in your line of fire instantly becomes aware of your coffee was prepared. Although you have just created a corroborating witness, you think better than to ask them for help in backing up your complaint. This unpleasant experience represents a knee-jerk reaction common to the non-Floridians in this country. Regardless of whether Jesus actually experienced this with a beverage, his simple analogy is a direct hit to the heart. Is this really the kind of reception we want from our Savior?

Growing up in the southern United States, I learned to apply names like "holy rollers" and "Bible thumpers" to people whose faith in God made them stand out wherever they went. These were the people who carried their Bibles with them, who spoke of Christ often, and who were at church every time the doors opened. In my mind, this behavior belonged to fanatics who went overboard, whereas I was doing ok as far as my faith was concerned. I knew all about the whole "lukewarm" thing and felt that it applied to people who were not as upstanding as myself. If you'd have asked me about this back then, I would have described a lukewarm Christian as one who did not read the Bible, who had no desire to attend church regularly, and who avoided discussions about God. Ironically, these three negative attributes described my life word per word. Only years later were my eyes opened to the lukewarm lifestyle I was living.

Today I feel it is without question that these individuals whose behavior I saw as excessive were being led by the love they had in their hearts for God; a love that grew from of their obedience to Him. Could it be that I knew this back then and simply whitewashed my own disobedience? I think yes, and no. While I was clearly making mental accommodations for my own desires, I was doing so without the knowledge of what those desires were supposed to be. Simply put, I felt I knew what the Bible said without having ever studied it. And what little I did know, I did nothing about.

Jesus held nothing back when it came to sharing his expectations that we become active and useful followers. If you're at all familiar with the red-letter text in your Bible, you'll know of his multiple attempts to hammer into the heads of his disciples that life cannot be lived on their terms. Even would-be disciples were informed of life adjustments that were required before they could join the group. Can you imagine approaching Jesus with the desire to follow him, only to be shown that your life, as is, is not worthy? I can't either. We'll take a look at such an encounter in a bit. Right now, I'd like you to meet a man whose life I fear too many of us will identify with.

3 American Idols

Meet Bob. Bob lives in Tennessee and is quite the football fan. His home is decorated with memorabilia of his home state's college team, as is his car and, on game day, even his dog whose name, "Pigskin" was cleverly chosen. When Bob is not attending a game or watching one at home, he stays occupied by reading various commentaries, studying player stats, and listening to podcasts concerning the team on his iPhone. On game day, Bob and his wife pride themselves on their friends' willingness to come to their home and enjoy the event on their super-sized TV. At the office, Bob is well known for his love of football and can be found discussing recent and upcoming games whenever he's not at his desk that, like his home, sports his team's colors and memorabilia.

At church, Bob is also seen as the go-to guy when it comes to engaging in conversations about football, which he does before Sunday school and during the break before the worship service. While Bob thoroughly enjoys hearing his pastor's sermons, he often finds himself preoccupied with the preparations he and his wife must make for the next gathering at their home to watch the big game. On these days, Bob never misses a chance to pray over the food he and his wife prepare for their friends and acts as a servant host to ensure the comfort of each of his guests. When the party is over, and the big screen is darkened, Bob retires to a much smaller screen while lying in bed where he can monitor the post-game activity and post his critique of various plays on Facebook after kissing his wife goodnight.

Bob sinks an enormous amount of time and energy into his own interests. There is no doubt that Bob has a heart for God. But his life reveals a much bigger heart for football, which is just one of the many things we can allow to take precedence over our relationship with Him. When we make them priority number one, we've totally missed commandment number one.

You shall have no other gods before Me.

Exodus 20:3

Right now, you're likely questioning how "gods" in this verse can refer to things like football, movies,

TV shows, scrapbooking, and cooking. After all, none of these are supreme beings. This is true. There may also be no formal worship ritual associated with any of them. Any of the countless activities we enjoy on earth, however, can indeed become gods or idols to us.

For the skeptics, consider all the things that God made. He made everything, right? Okay, He didn't necessarily construct the buildings in town or even the local churches, but nothing of which they were made was not first created by God. So, if we can agree that God did indeed create all things, we must equally agree upon what God did *not* create—other gods. So, where did the other gods that God speaks of come from? The answer is simple. We created them.

"Son of man, these men have set up idols in their hearts and put wicked stumbling blocks before their faces."

Ezekiel 14:3

Bear in mind that these things are not gods until we make them into gods. This process requires no real effort other than to grant them more of our love and attention than the commander of our love and attention who provided us with this life we so enjoy.

God created us for his own satisfaction. We exist because He wanted us to. And, just as any father or mother does, He wants us to regard Him as our parent and not share the love that is due Him with idols and earthly pleasures.

When we put God on the back burner in favor of a life lived on our own terms, we become like children whose willingness to come to dinner is contingent upon whether a tasty dessert will be served afterward. In the Bible, we read how thousands of potential followers of Jesus walked away when they found out that there would be no dessert. Those who stuck around did so knowing that not even dinner was guaranteed. Today, Jesus is still calling us to follow him. In the same way that God loves us unconditionally, our decision to follow must come with no conditions of our own.

The other day, my 12-year old daughter asked the question many of you as parents may have been asked. "In heaven, will there be stuff to do or will we just sit around worshipping God all day?" She obviously wanted to be sure that an earthly desire she had would be fulfilled eternally. I explained to her that heaven is not a place that transforms us from people who do not want to worship God all day into those who do. Rather, heaven is a *transition* for those who currently want to worship God all day. Despite my answer, her real question was not lost on me. She likely envisioned heaven as a continual worship service during which sitting still is not at all desirable. Her younger brother must doubly share this concern.

Our children's desire for this type of assurance is not unlike our own. As adults and youths, we too have tendencies to inquire much about the paths in life that are available to us before we choose to advance down any one of them. And there is one path in particular that I'd like us to explore next. It's one that both you and I have taken before and will likely take again.

4 Path of Least Resistance

We can't all be preachers. This statement is true. Indeed, not all of us are called to become leaders of a church. Nine times out of ten, however, this is not what is being declared. In these instances, a case is being made to support one's unwillingness to take on the duties of a Christian. Statements like these are made when one has no desire to put more than the minimal requirements into action. The larger the impact a chosen path stands to have on our lives, the less attractive it becomes.

During my rush hour commute, I often tune in to a Christian radio show that invites its listeners to call in with questions about the Bible. On one occasion, a man who announced his intent to prove his pastor wrong asked the question, "Is it really necessary to give ten percent of my earnings as a tithe?" Before I go any further, let me say that I have never wanted to be the host of a radio show more than I did on that day. A good friend of mine described himself as the "poster child for restraint" whenever he feared that weighing in on a situation would expose the level of reckless anxiety he was feeling. On this day, I was the kid on the poster as I listened to the radio host offer this caller exactly what he wanted to hear.

Without going into much detail, the host explained that tithing was not a requirement for one's salvation. To clarify, it was the host who skimped on the detail. There was much more about the dutiful act of tithing that he failed to discuss with this man. When the call ended, I felt the strong desire to call in myself and set the record straight. Instead, I made a good judgment call and decided not to butt in. My phone's battery being at 3% might have had something to do with it too. But mostly it was good judgment. Let's go with that.

This caller's attitude mirrors our own whenever we ponder over the things we can get away with not doing instead of anxiously seeking out all we can do to please God. Giving monetarily to our local churches is very much an act of obedience. It's just one of the many ways we can return thanks and express our adoration for God. Stopping after the minimum requirements is the same as denying Him a portion of our hearts. Imagine telling your fiancé that, if marriage required your love for only thirty years, you would be unwilling to go thirty-one. If this were a reality, I don't think you could expect the words, "I do" in your future. Even if you were eighty years old and weren't expected to live another thirty years, a partial heart is exactly that—not whole.

God feels the same way about the love we are to have for Him. And He has His own set of minimum requirements. They include *all* of our hearts, *all* of our souls, and *all* of our strength. Because the amount of love we have for Him will determine how obedient we will be to His instruction, we can be certain that partial obedience is not obedience at all. Jesus said that we must be willing to give up everything to become his disciples. The Bible relays this message in the story of the young rich man who asked Jesus how he might receive eternal life.

Jesus looked at him and loved him. "One thing you lack," he said. "Go, sell everything you have and give to the poor, and you will have treasure in heaven. Then come, follow me."

Mark 10:17-25

This guy didn't take Jesus' instruction very well. Instead of running off to do what he could to remain at Jesus' side, gloom over what he had to give up consumed his emotions as he walked away. He obviously was not willing to part with all his stuff. It was either that or the burden of having to create all those eBay auctions that overwhelmed him. Whatever the case, we do know that there's no record of this man ever catching up with Jesus and his disciples.

One thing we must keep in mind is that Jesus did not tell everyone they had to sell all their belongings. While this requirement appears in three of the four gospels, each recollection is about this same rich man. Others were required to hate their parents. We'll talk more about that one later. For now, just know that Jesus never told anyone who wished to follow him that they could not. Rather, he simply pointed out why they *would* not. His disciples had to be *willing* to go all-in or not go at all. Jesus himself demonstrated this commitment when he carried his cross. He did this willingly so that we would respond with a willingness to carry our own; not haggle over the smallest piece we can carry that can still be called a cross.

This *going all-in* requirement still applies today. In order to live life on Jesus' terms, we must first be willing to get rid of our own. For as long as we refuse, we too will not catch up to the group of disciples. And no one gets recognized as a Christian who isn't hanging with Jesus. Being recognized as a disciple is as crucial now as it was then. It's also just as difficult.

Looking up requires a constant effort to separate ourselves from this world; to stand out among those around us whose hearts are fixated on it. Jesus knew this would be an ongoing struggle for us, which is why he compared this hardship to his own. Granted, much of what we will face is nowhere near being in the same ballpark as Jesus' lugging a giant hunk of wood onto his bloodied and weakened back after being flogged. The vast majority of Christians will never come close to experiencing this type of suffering. But suffer we shall. Doing so simply comes with the territory of living a Christ-like life.

For you have been called for this purpose, since Christ also suffered for you, leaving you an example for you to follow in His steps . . .
1 Peter 2:21

As we learned in the first chapter, reactions to the burden each of us is expected to bear will differ from one person to the next. Some will actually welcome the load. To these, the burden associated with being a known follower of Jesus is a blessing regardless of its weight. Still, many will put forth a limited effort and even more will walk away at the mere sight of a challenge.

For every ounce of effort we put forth, there can be as many degrees of resistance along the paths we choose. The path of least resistance is simply the one we're all familiar with. I do know of another one though. It's called the path of *no* resistance. This path is not burdensome at all. No one will even know you chose it. Sound secret and hush-hush? It is. But you won't be traveling this path alone. There'll be plenty of people to rub shoulders with, including a young lady whom you'll get to know in the next chapter. If you recognize her, just know that she prefers to remain anonymous. She might even prefer to retain her *anonymity*, but I anticipate readers like me who have trouble saying that word. I even had to Google the correct spelling.

Did I say this was my first book?

5 Unspoken Word

Meet Kate. Kate is 27 years old and lives in small-town Louisiana. She arrived when she was 20 after her father became employed outside her home state of Texas. She promised herself on many occasions that she would return one day, but the bonds she made with several young ladies about her age made leaving unthinkable.

Often referred to as the "fearsome four," Kate and her three pals were anything but intimidating. In fact, the humility they displayed while serving those around them made these women stand out in their community. From baking treats for the neighborhood children to visiting elderly and homebound women, the love they showed others while together made a visit from these ladies something to look forward to. They were inseparable. Where one was, seeing the other three was almost a guarantee. There was, however, one place that you never saw them gather together.

Of the four, only Kate had made the decision to follow Jesus; only she had a different idea of what it meant to *follow* than Jesus did. In the years prior to making her home in Louisiana, Kate learned that being vocal about her faith only led to heated discussions during which she was often told to keep her Christian ideology to herself.

With this in hindsight, she wasn't about to cause a rift in this new life she so enjoyed by engaging others about Jesus. The respect she earned was too important to Kate to become tarnished with a label like "Little Miss Christian." So, she attended church outside of her community and remained silent about her faith. She was quite successful at suppressing it too. In fact, if you weren't around to see her wearing a summer dress as she got into her car early Sunday mornings, you'd never suspect that she was a God-fearing woman.

Kate was totally at ease with this choice of hers. In her mind, salvation was a personal matter. She didn't have to announce it. She could adhere to the Ten Commandments and obey Jesus' teachings without actually naming Jesus as her motivation for doing so. But was she being completely obedient? Did she satisfy God's will? Something tells me that she didn't. That something is the Bible.

Kate's attitude toward her faith is shared by a great number of people whose idea of *looking up* includes not being seen doing it. Many with this attitude contend that God's work will be accomplished whether we get involved or not. And it will be. God's will shall be done regardless, but His will includes our being active and outspoken disciples as Jesus informs us in these next few verses.

Then Jesus came to them and said, "All authority in heaven and on earth has been given to me. Therefore go and make disciples of all nations, baptizing them in the name of the Father and of the Son and of the Holy Spirit, and teaching them to obey everything I have commanded you. And surely I am with you always, to the very end of the age."

Matthew 28:18-20

Jesus invested a great deal of time and energy into his twelve disciples so that they would go into the world and create more. They did this by delivering the message of the gospel. Those who would become new disciples were to make a commitment to do the same. We are all called to become disciples. But only those who are committed will become one.

If you're concerned that discipleship will not be easy, you're in good company. It wasn't easy for Paul and John, nor was it for the rest of the disciples. And it's not expected to be easy for us. But it is no less God's instruction for our lives; an instruction that, if followed, will have a huge impact on our own hearts as well as those around us. Jesus told us how we can accomplish this too—by loving one another. He said people will know we are his disciples if we do this.

A new commandment I give to you, that you love one another, even as I have loved you, that you also love one another. By this all men will know that you are My disciples, if you have love for one another.

John 13:34-35

The concern over Kate's life is not her lack of love. Her actions clearly revealed the passion she had for serving others. The concern is that her friends who were not Christians were equally showing love to those around them, and Kate simply blended in. So, how are we supposed to stand out among non-believers who lend their efforts to help the homeless, provide love and care for children, and who are equally kind to their neighbors? The answer is in the verse you just read.

Take a moment to examine Jesus' words. In fact, take a few while I run and grab a Dr. Pepper.

I'm back. I took a little longer than expected. Two days in fact. Hopefully, you got the picture and weren't sitting and waiting this whole time. If you need a refresher, take another moment to read over those last few verses. I'm not going anywhere this time, I promise. There are three words that will help us to better understand this instruction. The three I'm referring to are "as I have." Per Jesus, we aren't just supposed to love; we're to love as he did. And how exactly did he love his disciples, you ask? He did it with kindness, patience, and sympathy. More importantly though, Jesus loved them with his words.

An incredible love was demonstrated through Jesus' teaching of God's love for them and of His will for their lives. They came to know God through Jesus, just the way we do. So, while we can love our neighbors, pray for our enemies, and learn to forgive as Jesus did, doing so without naming Jesus' life, death, and resurrection as our motivators may hinder our ability to be seen as anything but good people. Simply put, nothing says, "I love Jesus" like saying, "I love Jesus." Shouting it is equally effective. If you get a warm fuzzy feeling when you do this, it's because your heart hears you. And so does Jesus.

Whoever acknowledges me before others, I will also acknowledge before my Father in heaven.

Matthew 10:32

As Christians, we are in the soul-winning business. Our salvation is merely the beginning of the incredible journey that God has prepared for us. This journey requires significant action on our part. Before we hit the streets though, we must have a firm understanding of our marching orders. Without this knowledge, we're like salespeople with no clue about the product we're selling. This brings to mind a recent encounter with a cable TV rep who was "in the neighborhood" selling fifty-seven channels with nothing on. Nothing on *TV* that is. He wasn't naked, thank God.

6 Required Reading

Something I have found to be common among men is our tendency to ignore the instruction manuals that come with the things we buy. We'll even refuse to listen when the ladies in our lives who, upon detecting our operating struggles, will grab the instructions themselves and read them aloud. I just checked my thesaurus for an antonym of *fun* to describe when ladies do this, but none of the words I found matched the strength of this feeling without using compound adverbs. Highly extremely unpleasant this is.

As a drummer of many years, I chose to invest in a set of electronic drums to play in my home. Having watched several demo videos on YouTube while awaiting their arrival on the big brown truck, I was confident in my ability to operate the drums' sound module with no assistance. I'd played these types of drums before, so I gave the lengthy instruction manual no attention. It wasn't going to teach me anything I didn't know, or so I thought.

After enjoying my drums for several months, I found myself unable to make them do something that I knew they were capable of. After two days of trial and error, I gave up and reluctantly dug the instruction manual from beneath the foam packing trays in the giant box that the drums came in.

As I scanned the table of contents, I became stunned to learn of a feature I wished I'd known about when the drums first arrived. This wasn't some new sound that I discovered. No, it was much bigger than that. To me, activating this feature would be like having a whole new drum set. When I told a drumming buddy about my discovery, my excitement was met with an underwhelming response. Apparently, this feature was common knowledge among drummers. Even so, he agreed that I had only been experiencing half of what my new drums could do. My wife was also underwhelmed when I informed her, but not because she already knew about it.

If there's one thing I've learned about marriage, it's that wives will never share enthusiasm over their husbands' newfound gadget functionality. If you're a husband and get so much as a "that's nice, dear," you can be sure your wife is really pondering over why you haven't fixed the toilet. If I jogged your memory about an item on your honey-do list, you're welcome to pause and go take care of it. The rest of us will place bets on whether you'll ever make back. We've lost some good men this way.

Just as instruction manuals are created to teach us how to use our phones, dishwashers, and sewing machines, the Bible was written to serve as a guide for life on earth. While ignoring instructions for appliances can result in our opening the wrong side of a can of green beans, consequences of ignoring the Bible can lead to fates worse than death. What can be worse than death? According to a poll that was designed to determine what people fear the most, public speaking is worse. But I was referring to the place those who have no regard for life's instruction manual go after they die. The high likelihood of there being no public speaking going on in this place is not a reason to breathe easy. In fact, breathing easy will just as likely not occur.

I'm not saying that hell is reserved for all who do not read their Bibles. I do, however, do feel certain that none of hell's residents will be in possession of the most crucial benefit that being reliant upon Scripture provides—a relationship with God. We'll learn more about this relationship as we go along together. For now, I'd like us to explore reasons why so many of us are apt to ignore our God-given instruction manual.

The first reason is the one we just discussed. Our Bibles often remain untouched because we feel they will provide nothing we don't already know. We'll open them to follow along with our preacher on Sunday mornings when he asks us to, but then shelve our Bibles for the remainder of the week. Another reason is that many of us feel the Bible is just too darn big. This reason often accompanies the claim that it's too tough to understand. There are only so many *thees, thous,* and *begats* we can stomach, right? Sympathizers with this outlook often regard reading Scripture as a hassle or an inconvenience that stands to interrupt their busy lifestyles.

Next, we have our procrastinators. Having been one myself, I know this group all too well. Procrastinators will not dismiss the importance of reading the Bible. They know how vital it is to our lives, but there will always to be time to study it. While both death and the rapture stand to rob us of that time, the procrastinator sees neither as an immediate threat. Thus, reading the Bible is not an immediate need. And so tomorrow becomes the more attractive option for beginning the journey into God's Word. It should also be noted that people who claim the Bible is too tough to comprehend are often hiding amongst this group. Their cover is blown after being given a more readable translation that remains untouched.

There are indeed many things we can achieve without reading the instructions. Obedience to God, however, is not one of them. Having Google at our disposal to find a verse when we need one is very handy, but knowing only snippets of the Bible does not relieve us of our need for the knowledge of God's Word in its entirety. Yes, this instruction manual is quite large. But our devotion to the Bible guarantees the continual discovery of new life features that we'll wish we'd known about a long time ago.

This list of attitudes toward Scripture is by no means comprehensive. In fact, there is yet another outlook that lends itself to becoming spiritually dormant. It belongs to those who feel that their destination was reached when they became saved and that there is nothing more required of us. We'll examine this mindset in the next chapter, which is currently without a title. I still haven't come up with a name for it yet. Hopefully, I'll have chosen a good one before you turn the page.

7 Mission Accomplished?

Ok, so the title's not very creative. But it does reflect a question that many of us stand to ask ourselves. When we set our sights on something we want, we begin to feel anxious about it, especially if it's not immediately available to us. Let's say you just read an announcement for a new gadget or household item that does something none of the items you currently own can do, or can do quite as well. You'd love to have this functionality right away, but you have to wait for it to hit the market. Things like movie trailers do this for us. That's why they're called *teasers*. While a few months' wait for a new movie is expected, directors whose teaser trailers announce their films half a year in advance should be slapped. Why do this to us? If the force doesn't get unleashed until December, why tell us about it in June?

Anyway, when the wait is finally over, and we've gotten the item or seen the movie we'd been waiting for, something within each of us changes.

All the anxiety we once felt is replaced by mere satisfaction over the newly acquired. And this satisfaction becomes mundane as what was once new and exciting becomes an everyday thing or something we merely reflect on as having been there and done that. The resurgence of our anxiety, however, is imminent as our next target is never far away. In other words, when we finally get what we've been looking forward to or achieve what we set out to accomplish, it is our nature as humans to fix our gaze on something else.

Now for the big question. Why should we continue to seek Christ when we already have salvation in our back pocket? The book of Matthew answers this question. We carry on because we are in love with Jesus.

Then Jesus said to His disciples, "If anyone wishes to come after Me, he must deny himself, and take up his cross and follow Me."

Matthew 16:24

Here Jesus teaches us about those who will "come after," or *pursue* him. In chapter 4, we explored what it means to take up our cross. This is not meant to be a one-time event. Rather, it's what is expected of us continually throughout our lives. Just as Jesus was driven by love for us to give up his life, we are to become driven by this same love for him and press on amidst whatever hardships our chosen path takes us through.

Do you remember the days and months that followed your first encounter with the person you married or hope to marry? Do you remember the heart-pounding desire you had? It's likely that you never wanted anything more than you did him or her at that time. I bet you can also recall your anxiety going into overdrive when life's obstacles kept you apart.

For some, these obstacles may have been as mild as a distant drive, while others may have involved military obligations that kept you apart far longer than you were willing to be. Whatever the circumstance, it was no match for your heart. Love was the driving force that kept you actively and anxiously in pursuit of that person.

If you are experiencing this now, you likely aren't reading this book. You're probably at the movies together, enjoying dinner, or out hiking near a lake; whatever feeds that desire you have for your true love. One thing I am certain of is that you are *not stopping*. Noth—

Hey! I heard that! Someone just shouted, "That happens *after* you get married!" It sounded like it was coming from the Carolinas. Very funny. Just so you know, your chapter is coming. By the way, if any of you know how to insert one of those evil grin smiley emojis, let me know.

Ok, where was I? Oh right, the part about not stopping. When we became saved, we received a gift that allows us to receive guidance and personal communication from Jesus. This gift is God's Holy Spirit, who we'll discuss further in the next chapter. This is what people are talking about when they say that Jesus is living inside us. Receipt of this gift marks the beginning of an incredible one-on-one relationship we can have with Christ. Why on earth would we want to quit now? As crazy as it may seem, people do. Here's a quick story that will help us through the remainder of this chapter.

The humidity was thick on an afternoon in June as three female track and field runners arrived to participate in an Olympic trial event. In this trial, the top three runners would become Olympians in the next Summer Games. Upon her arrival, Jenny Reed's high tension turned to perplexity when learned that she would be competing with only two ladies instead of five. There would be no delayed or rescheduled trial for the absentees. This was it. The three future Olympians would be selected by default.

When it was announced that the competition would commence, each of the ladies finished stretching their muscles and proceeded to their starting positions. But when the starter pistol was fired, only two of the ladies sprinted forward. Instead of running, Jenny walked slowly to the side of the track and sat down in the grass.

When the race was over, the participants were led to a banquet area in the stadium where news reporters were waiting to photograph and interview the future Olympians. This area was reserved for VIP events and was decorated for this momentous occasion. As Jenny entered with the other ladies, she was pulled aside by the master of ceremonies.

"What are you doing?" the man asked. Jenny explained that, since there were only three who showed up, the decision was locked in. She couldn't lose, so she opted not to waste her energy. Jenny was then advised that the decision was to be made over the top "finishers," and, because she did not run, she could not be selected. At this, Jenny became distraught and began to argue her many months of preparation for this opportunity. "I earned this!" she cried. But there was nothing that could persuade the man who denied Jenny's participation in the honoree ceremony and asked her to leave.

Just as Jenny was certain things would go her way, there will be many whose beliefs that they are saved will one day be crushed. Our master of ceremonies describes this day in the book of Matthew.

Not everyone who says to me, 'Lord, Lord,' will enter the kingdom of heaven, but the one who does the will of my Father who is in heaven. On that day many will say to me, 'Lord, Lord, did we not prophesy in your name, and cast out demons in your name, and do many mighty works in your name?' And then will I declare to them, 'I never knew you; depart from me, you workers of lawlessness.'

Matthew 7:21-23

In what have been called the scariest verses in the Bible, Jesus draws the line between those who will receive salvation and those who will be denied it. That line is a relationship with him. Casting out demons and prophesying were the equivalent of the arguments we might make today. Didn't I believe? Didn't I go forward in church? Didn't I get baptized?

In terms of a race, our having done each of these activities merely places us at the starting line. We can be suited up and ready to go, but the effort is worthless if we don't run.

Each of us is to pursue Jesus continually using the same energy we put into our relationships with each other. When we do, we have the guarantee that he will never brush us off the way a beautiful brunette in the tenth grade with blue eyes and freckles, and who thought herself better than to be seen in public with the likes of you will have done. What? This didn't happen to you too in high school? Surely one of you can sympathize with me. After all, she dissed a lot of guys.

Anyway, back to Jesus. Even when he alerts us to the things in our lives that stand to hinder our pursuit as he did with the rich man, he never ceases to meet us with open arms. And he'd love nothing more than to be seen with us everywhere we go. But do we equally want to be seen with *him*? Believe it or not, Jesus gets dissed too.

8 Holy Communication

As avid cell phone users, we all have a good idea about what we want from a service plan. While shopping, we look for the terms, *unlimited* and *uninterrupted* as they describe the features that make these plans so attractive. While unlimited features are great, uninterrupted service is far more important as interruptions can limit the unlimited. We also look at coverage areas to ensure service exists everywhere we imagine ourselves being. Whether we're shopping for pigs in New Guinea or for shepherds in Germany, we'd like to know we can call home to make sure our lawn elves are still in order. Finally, we do a little research to determine how well the carrier holds up their end of the bargain. This is where those user reviews that we all love to read come into play.

What many shoppers fail to realize is that the ratio of satisfied customers who do not feel led to sound off online about their experiences to those who do leans significantly toward the happy silent people. Those with bad experiences, on the other hand, are twice as likely to go online and voice a negative opinion. As a result, the number of stars given to a product based on user input may not accurately reflect how well consumers are receiving it. I know I'm veering off course a bit, but this is a fun topic. Speaking of fun topics, I had to resist the urge to include "Batman" in the title of this chapter. Yes, I'm a nerd.

So, we love our phones, and we sink a good bit of our time end energy toward the assurance of continued clear and unobstructed communication. Jesus wants to have this same quality of communication with us. His attempts to reach us, however, are often jammed with obstructions that we create while under the impression that he stopped speaking long ago. In these verses, Jesus assures us that the opposite is true.

"I have many more things to say to you, but you cannot bear them now. But when He, the Spirit of truth, comes, He will guide you into all the truth; for He will not speak on His own initiative, but whatever He hears, He will speak; and He will disclose to you what is to come. He will glorify Me, for He will take of mine and will disclose it you."

John 16:12-14

In the previous chapter, we learned a bit about the Holy Spirit's provision of guidance for our lives. According to Jesus, being in possession of the Holy Spirit was actually better for his disciples than for him to remain with them.

I tell you the truth, it is to your advantage that I go away; for if I do not go away, the Helper will not come to you; but if I go, I will send Him to you.

John 16:7

In this verse, Jesus referred to the Holy Spirit as a "helper." And his departure from earth was necessary for them to have it. Jesus also used the pronoun, "Him" in his description of the Holy Spirit. In case you haven't already guessed, *He* is God. And we need not look further than our hearts and minds for His guidance that we have unlimited access to. No smartphone needed.

One of the drawbacks to reading the typed word is that one cannot always detect the amount of enthusiasm the writer intends to portray. Such is the case in this instance. I could type in all caps or use a phrase like, "freakin' awesome," which actually captures my feelings toward this quite well.

Instead, I'll try to retain a bit of reverence and use *incomprehensible* and *incredible*; two words that are frequently used to describe God's love for us. Having the Holy Spirit at the helm of our attention each day is indeed incredible. And yet so many of us turn our attention to other things and essentially bury Jesus' signal, thus interrupting the unlimited.

To recall the term, *incomprehensible*, it is this that one would choose to bury the presence of the Holy Spirit. But it happens more often than you might think. Imagine that your neighbor inherited a vintage sports car that would make any car enthusiast drool; maybe one of those Aston Martins that Sean Connery drove in the early Bond films. Now picture your reaction to your neighbor's decision to keep this car underneath a tarp inside his garage, never taking it out for any reason. Wouldn't that just drive you batty? I'm guessing that you could never look at your neighbor's house again without wondering why something so precious was given absolutely no attention. If it were me who received this spectacular vehicle, I'd certainly show it off. I might even get a tuxedo like Connery's to wear while driving it. Well, maybe more like Daniel Craig's, but I would certainly have some fun with the car before selling it to Jay Leno.

Jesus told us about the things we can do to be attentive to the gift of the Holy Spirit. These include reading God's word daily, praying regularly, loving our neighbors as ourselves, and having no idols in our lives that consume our thoughts, desires, and our energy. Each of these efforts stands to increase the clarity of his communication. It's when we allow things like sports, video games, TV shows, and other interests to rule our attention that Jesus' signal becomes undetected. It is when we store bitterness toward others within our hearts that our focus is drawn away from God. And it is when we are not seeking God through His word that our earthly desires take precedence over His.

Achieving the optimum signal between the Holy Spirit and us is essential to a life lived looking up. Removing all the static is no easy task. God, however, upon seeing our hearts' desire for a clear signal, will guide and assist our efforts. Details of God's service plan can be found in the books of the Bible from Genesis to Revelation. It's guaranteed to be uninterrupted with unlimited service for life. I think I'll go ahead and end this chapter now to stifle any further corny analogies about the lack of an activation fee. That and unlimited text. That one's about the Bible. Get it?

9 Good Mythical Marriage

In Chapter 7, we used the romantic relationship as a model for the love we are to have for Jesus. As we develop this same love for one another, our minds become fixated on the idea of marriage. Let's talk about that. Singles, please don't head out for coffee and doughnuts just yet. I promise this will be valuable to your relationships as well. Maybe we can all take a trip to Krispy Kreme when we've finished the last chapter. For now, let's focus on what some of us affectionately refer to as "the M-word."

I'll begin with what I believe to be the most profound statement in this book. Here goes. The institution of marriage was created to glorify God. Ok, maybe that statement isn't so much profound as it is profoundly different from what we believe marriage is supposed to be. Either way, nothing could be more accurate about this union. The roles of husbands and wives were designed specifically to bring honor to God, who created all things to work in the same manner. And yes, "all things" includes you and me.

So, if each one of us was created to bring glory to God, then it goes without saying that everything we do should accomplish this, so long as we do it right. And the book of Ephesians sheds some light on how marriage is done right.

Wives, be subject to your own husbands, as to the Lord. For the husband is the head of the wife, as Christ also is the head of the church, He Himself being the Savior of the body. But as the church is subject to Christ, so also the wives ought to be to their husbands in everything.

Ephesians 5:22-24

In these verses, to be "subject to" is to be *submissive*, which is not a popular word in our world, especially when it pertains to wives. This is due to the common misconception that a submissive wife is stripped of her voice and of her value within a marriage. Before we clear the air about what it means to be submissive in marriage, let's read about the role of the husband.

Husbands, love your wives, just as Christ also loved the church and gave Himself up for her, so that He might sanctify her . . .

Ephesians 5:25-26

Wives are indeed to be submissive to their husbands in everything. But this submission is to be subject to a husband who, in turn, is submissive to his wife's every need. It's when these roles are misunderstood that they bear the negative labels we slap on them. You've likely encountered this role confusion at some point. Husbands who abuse their leadership and wives who order their passive husbands around only confirm that marriage doesn't always play out the way it's supposed to. Further evidence can be seen in the statistical data concerning the rate of divorce among Christians in the United States.

If there's anything I've learned to take with a grain of salt, it's statistics. The results of polls these days are just as likely to have been skewed to suit varying agendas as they are to reflect solid and useful data. I was, however, able to draw a solid conclusion about these results without having to scrub for accuracy. It is that they lead Americans to *believe* Christian couples divorce just as often as non-Christian couples do. And, because it is understood that Christian behavior is deep-rooted in Scripture, it may also be concluded that Christians who divorce simply aren't reading it.

Back to our instructions, a major factor in our unwillingness to refer to them is pride. We lose a little of that pride when we come to terms with the inability do things on our own. I'm placing this topic on the stand during our next chapter as the effects of pride extend well beyond the walls of marriage. This is a good place to start though. We can even start with my own if you want. Alright, let me think. When am I prideful? Ok, I've got one. For the record, this one was pulled from a very large hat filled to the brim with examples I could share with you.

When I go to Walmart with a specific item in mind to buy whose location in the store is uncharted territory, the last thing I want to do is ask someone where it is. My shopping mission is not a successful one if I lose out on the discovery experience. My wife does not share my sense of adventure in the retail jungle and spoils these missions by asking for help if I take longer than the few minutes her patience allows. This is why I prefer to shop alone! To give her at least some credit, I have indeed been known to turn a quick run for milk and butter into a two-hour excursion. But I always get what is needed, even if I have to spend an hour at the PlayStation kiosk to get it. A man's gotta do what a man's gotta do!

While I'm willing to admit that my silly pride keeps

me from asking for assistance, there is a point where I'll break down and ask. It would be foolish of me to leave without the item I came for if I knew that item existed in the store. And it would be equally foolish to ask another shopper for help finding it instead of the clerk who is trained to point me in the right direction. After all, the clerk has intimate knowledge of the store layout whereas another customer may be as clueless as I am.

If we were to turn this example into a parable, a successful marriage would be the item being sought, and the married couple would serve as the customer who's looking for it. As for the clerk, he would be God who has intimate knowledge of both marriage and its whereabouts. And we'll let the other shopper be the Dr. Phil's of the world who are known to point people in the wrong direction. This would actually be a good parable if I hadn't left out a key character. I failed to reference the many Christian couples who never even make it to the store before ending their marriages in divorce.

Of the couples who do make an effort to resolve their differences, many seek worldly solutions via magazine articles, talk shows, and by using other couples as models for their relationship. While I do enjoy watching Dr. Phil, sometimes his marital advice has more potential to steer couples into a downward spiral toward divorce than to guide them away from it. This is due to the popular notion that marital bliss is achieved through personal happiness.

The problem with this idea is that husbands and wives each have varying views of what makes them happy. When both become reluctant to sacrifice any portion of that happiness, common ground is seldom reached. The split occurs when one or both spouses feel they can no longer count on the marriage for the happiness they deserve. If they had only referred to the instruction manual, they would know that the fulfillment they seek is not to come from each other, but from God.

For you singles who are reading this, you may want to re-evaluate what you desire most in a potential groom or bride. Should you look for someone who can ultimately meet your personal desires or should a spouse compliment your desire to seek God above all else? And shouldn't you already be in a committed relationship with Him when you get married? After all, choosing the one you'll be spending your remaining days on earth with is pretty important. You might as well do it right.

Also, don't let the Carolina chatter you heard earlier convince you that marriage isn't wonderful. Don't expect perfection either. You'll still squabble over your differences. But if you love as Jesus loves, and if you forgive each other as God forgave you, there's nothing your relationship will not endure. When our marriages are deep-rooted in forgiveness, we can move beyond the bumps we encounter and get back to focusing on the reason we are together in the first place—glorifying God.

Whew! That was a tough chapter. I had originally written two but ended up merging them into one. Given the number of years we spend in matrimony, the topic is worthy of the thousands of chapters you can read in other books dedicated to the institution marriage. Just be sure to read the book that is the ultimate authority on marriage first if you're planning on shopping for one. It's the one book you should never judge by its cover.

Since I've already introduced the next topic, now would be a good time to set your book down and stretch for a moment. I'm certainly going to. I don't actually *have* a book to set down though.

Wait for it . . .

10 A Prideful People

As we move through our days and years, we make mental notes to ourselves for various reasons. If we could mouse-click on our brains, we would see a series of file folders that we create to categorize these notes. The folder names will vary a bit from brain to brain, but most can be found inside every head. The folder I'd like for us to examine today is the one labeled, "Things I Will Not Do." You may want to sort your folders alphabetically if you can't find it right away. When you open it, you'll find a number of subfolders, each named for a reason you will not do something. Inside these are where our notes are stored. The number of folders and notes we store tend to go up and down from time to time as we experience new things and change our minds about our blacklisted items. Some notes get moved to other folders while others get deleted entirely.

Just for fun, I'll open one of my notes. Ok, this one says that I will not, under any circumstances, eat sushi. I can assure you that I have no plans to remove that one. It's in my "Icky/Gross" subfolder that I'm sure you have as well. Next to that folder is one labeled, "It's Beneath Me." Double-click on this one if you will. Each note in this folder describes actions we will not perform in front of other people. If you've ever referred to one of these actions, you may have used the term, *stooping*.

Stooping is an action that we fear will negatively affect the opinions others have of us. An example might be a well-paid lawyer's refusal to drive a Hyundai or clean offices for a living should he or she become unemployed. Another might reflect a socialite's unwillingness to consort with a person due to their inferior social standing. This hesitancy to stoop that we have is the result of pride. Your "Pride" folder is in your brain's root directory. Many of the notes we file away are automatically copied to this folder for our convenience. Don't bother trying to open it though. Access is heavily protected by our hearts' firewall.

The Gospel of Luke paints a picture of a prostitute who did what many of us would call stooping. One afternoon, she watched as Jesus visited the home of a well-to-do man named Simon. Knowing she would not be welcome inside due to her reputation, this woman's longing for Jesus clouded all else as she entered and fell down before him. While sobbing uncontrollably, the woman took what was left of her pride and poured it on Jesus' feet. Pride, in her case, was in the form of a little bottle filled with perfume that dangled from her necklace. She likely wore this perfume in order to feel clean as she walked among those who regarded her as a nasty harlot.

If you recall reading this story or discussing it during Sunday school, you may not have been informed that women were treated as the lesser of the two sexes during this period. In fact, divorced women were widely considered damaged goods even if it was the husband's indiscretion that caused the couple to split. As a result, many divorced women who were not taken in as slaves resorted to prostitution in order to survive on their own. While the Bible does not inform us of this woman's circumstance, her shattered heart over the life she led is fully realized. When the bottle was emptied, the woman began to kiss Jesus' feet while sopping up her tears with her own hair.

This woman showed us what it means to be broken before God. All concern over her dignity took a back seat to this man who would soon allow himself to be tortured and killed for her. So, what could she have known about this Jesus that made her act this way?

She knew that he offered the love and forgiveness that was not available to her anywhere else. This man was surely the Savior he claimed to be. When Simon saw what was happening, he assured Jesus that he would not have let her touch him at all had he known the kind of person she was. What Jesus said to Simon in return was priceless.

Then he turned toward the woman and said to Simon, "Do you see this woman? I came into your house. You did not give me any water for my feet, but she wet my feet with her tears and wiped them with her hair. You did not give me a kiss, but this woman, from the time I entered, has not stopped kissing my feet. You did not put oil on my head, but she has poured perfume on my feet. Therefore, I tell you, her many sins have been forgiven—as her great love has shown. But whoever has been forgiven little loves little." Then Jesus said to her, "Your sins are forgiven."

Luke 7:44-48

Later on, we read how Jesus himself stooped to do for his disciples what this woman had done for him. The Son of Man knelt before his friends and washed their dirty feet. He then dried their feet using his own robe as a towel. Afterward, Jesus urged these men to do likewise for each other in order to demonstrate what he called the second greatest commandment—to love one another. This, of course, was in light of the greatest commandment that we love our Lord, God with all our hearts, souls, and minds.

Throughout Scripture, love is at the forefront of every lesson we encounter. It is commanded by God that we possess and express this love that He had for an eternity before humanity was ever a thing. It is as much a law that we love as it is that we not steal, lie, or covet. We only have to turn on the news to see what happens in the absence of this love.

Because lawlessness is increased, most people's love will grow cold. But the one who endures to the end, he will be saved.
Matthew 24:12-13

In this verse, Jesus names "lawlessness" as the culprit for a rise in coldheartedness at the time of the end. At the same time, cold hearts are what's fueling this lawlessness. So, there's a double entendre here. You might even call it a double *tundra*. You know, because we're talking about the cold. Yes, I'll be here all week.

Any way you choose slice my cheesy humor, it's understood that followers of Jesus are guaranteed to have a tough road ahead. As the world increasingly reflects the lawlessness Jesus spoke of, we must ask ourselves if we can endure. The question, however, is not whether we can live through this. Rather, can we *love* through this? This is the struggle Jesus was talking about. Can we love one another in a world that insights hatred in our hearts? Can we pray for those who oppress us as lovers of Christ? Can our hearts remain fixated on God above all earthly distractions? Can we be merciful to those who put the killing of our brothers and sisters in Christ on display for the world to see? Can we love through this? Salvation awaits those who will until the very end.

Today, Jesus' example of how we should love one another is often shunned in fear of what we feel others will believe about us. We dare not stoop the way he did, lest our confidence suffer a major hit. When did preserving our self-image become so important? Determining *when* may be a tough hill to climb. So, in the next chapter, we'll take the easier route and explore *why* we allow our own will to prevail over God's.

11 Out of This World

To prepare for this chapter, take a moment or two and reflect on who or what you feel has made the greatest impact on your life. Typical answers to this question include one's parents, a teacher, music, and the Bible. These are our influences that shape the way we see the world. Despite having countless varieties, influences can be grouped into two categories — *worldly* and *Godly*.

Worldly influences spark the desire in us to become better aligned with our culture and the people we interact with regularly. Godly influence drives us toward pleasing God and achieving His will for our lives. Because our influences have a dramatic effect on our behavior, those who know us can attest to their impact on our daily routines. In the case of worldly influence, many who come to feel they are inadequately paired with the culture's standards will take measures to eliminate this feeling; sometimes drastic measures.

Take, for instance, a woman who decides to undergo voluntary cosmetic surgery to enhance her physical appearance. Her decision to do this may be influenced by popular media and social trends that suggest the need for her to become more pleasing to others than she is in her current state. If so, her motivation is the result of worldly influence. This is but one example among the many non-surgical efforts we make each day to better fit in with the world around us. Let's now read together a selection from the book of 1st John regarding these motives.

Do not love the world or the things in the world. If anyone loves the world, the love of the Father is not in him. For all that is in the world - the desires of the flesh and the desires of the eyes and pride of life - is not from the Father but is from the world. And the world is passing away along with its desires, but whoever does the will of God abides forever.

1 John 2:15-17

Here John defines the essence of looking up. He advises that the focal points of our hearts and minds should not be fixed on maintaining our acceptance here, but on our acceptance in heaven. He does this by contrasting the amount of time we will spend on earth against the amount of time we will spend in heaven. I recall hearing a similar comparison years ago. It was said that the difference between time on earth and in heaven would be like comparing something barely detectable under an electron microscope with the scope of our entire universe. This, of course, is an unfair comparison as the infinite element is represented by a finite one. But it's how we think as humans. Eternity is not something our minds can comprehend. And one day, it will be the earth that we cannot comprehend. In heaven, our entire recollection of this place will be erased.

See, I will create new heavens and a new earth. The former things will not be remembered, nor will they come to mind.

Isaiah 65:17

As compelling as this truth may be, time cannot motivate a heart the way love can. Our love for God is what causes this separation to occur. Our attitudes and behaviors will begin to change as we come to have an overwhelming desire to be with our Savior. Just as our friends know when we've fallen in love with another person, our love for God, when fed properly, will be easily detected.

Imagine a world where Jesus' followers walked with twelve inches of air between their feet and the ground. Feel free to dress them up in neon green as well. Yes, you may use hot pink instead. Also, if your imaginary world is under twelve inches of snow, you may want to raise Christians to twenty-four inches. Put elf shoes on them if you want. Just make sure they are the furthest thing from blending in as possible. Minus the silliness, the scope of this example mirrors the way we all should stand out as followers of Christ. We may not hover above the ground, but the way we walk will indeed reveal the Godly influence in our lives.

. . . walk in a manner worthy of the Lord, to please Him in all respects, bearing fruit in every good work and increasing in the knowledge of God.

Colossians 1:10

In this verse, "walk" is used to describe our day-to-day behavior. You've likely heard someone speak of their "walk with Christ." This person is referring to their life; a life that is equal to literally having a Hebrew man wearing a white robe and sandals accompany you everywhere you go. If shown a picture of the two of you walking together through Walmart, anyone could pick out who doesn't belong. Ok, Jesus might

actually blend in at Walmart, but you get the picture.

Each of us is charged with the task of not blending in with the world. This happens for us when the Godly influence in our lives begins to override the worldly. While those who know us can certainly tell which influence has the greater impact on us, we can know for ourselves without having to ask them. Here's how.

Take a few minutes to reflect on your daily routine. There is likely one activity you take part in more than any other. This will not be something you simply do often. Rather, it will be what you can't imagine doing without. If you've got one singled out, consider the number of hours each week you spend engaging in, planning for, and just thinking about this activity. Depending on how important it is to you, it may be the one thing that you will not allow any other activity to interfere with. If this activity is something other than Bible study, prayer, worship, or lending your talents to serve God, consider swapping your thing with one like these that launches or escalates your pursuit of a relationship with Him.

Take note of what's going on inside your heart as you do this. If you're experiencing a negative reaction, you may have just confirmed that worldly influence has the tighter grip on your heart.

If you were not able to pinpoint an activity for this test, don't worry. You can still take it. Instead of reflecting on all that you do, just take note of what you don't do. Either way, a swap may be in order. Only you can know if it is. And only you can do something about it. That young rich guy took this same test and failed miserably when he decided not to make the swap that his life needed. If you found that yours has this need, feel free to use his test as a cheat sheet. Just don't match his answers. Lastly, keep in mind that merely swapping activities has no bearing on your final grade. All set? You may begin.

12 Credible Witness

It's a beautiful July morning as you slip on your running shoes and head out to enjoy your regular jog. While moving through the park, you spot a woman sitting on a bench whose face you recognize. You can't place her right away, so you decide to get a better look at her during your next lap. When she comes into view, you recognize her as the host of the "Clean Living" TV show; a local program promoting healthy nutrition and protecting the environment. As you approach her during your third lap, you plan to stop and say hello, but keep running when you see that she's eating a Phat Burger, which is known to be the greasiest fast food in town. "How can she be eating that?" you ask yourself. As you round the corner a fourth time, you see her toss the burger wrapper on the ground and walk away.

Now, there are two ways you can react to this situation. You can let her poor choices slide in favor of the strong values she promotes, or you dismiss her claim to those values upon seeing her actions that clearly contradict them. I think it's safe to say that we would all do the latter.

As much as we care about how others see us, we often pay too little attention to what others see us *doing*. To keep us honest, the Bible addresses our many behaviors and urges us to be continually aware of how we perform them. Our teacher for this chapter will be the Apostle Paul whose lesson for us spans multiple books. We'll look at the one called Philippians first.

Do all things without grumbling or disputing; so that you will prove yourselves to be blameless and innocent, children of God above reproach in the midst of a crooked and perverse generation . . .

Philippians 2:14-15

In this fiftieth book of our Bible, Paul urges us not to place mud in the hands of those who are prone to sling it. The essence of this sentiment lies in the context of the word, *reproach* which refers to the expression of disapproval. For Christians, a reproach occurs when we are called out for behavior that conflicts with the Bible's teachings. Being *above* reproach requires our not giving anyone reason to question the authenticity and sincerity of our faith. Our friend, the TV host seemed to be struggling with this one.

Have you ever heard someone with a foul mouth claim to love Jesus? I sure have. And I'm certain I won't be hitting that person up for Godly advice anytime soon. But what if this person wasn't murdering the English language? What if this individual was just enjoying a glass of wine while expressing adoration for our Lord? Should wine be reason enough to discard one's effectiveness as a witness for Christ? Let's find out.

Among its multitude of life lessons, the Bible uses alcohol consumption as an example on numerous occasions. There are many hard stances that people take on this issue. God, however, takes only one. Let's look at it together. In the book of Ephesians, Paul writes:

Be very careful, then, how you live - not as unwise but as wise, making the most of every opportunity, because the days are evil. Therefore do not be foolish, but understand what the Lord's will is. Do not get drunk on wine, which leads to debauchery. Instead, be filled with the Spirit, speaking to one another

with psalms, hymns, and songs from the Spirit.

Ephesians 5:15-21

Have you ever wondered why God's decree against drunkenness never carried any weight with our Congress? We have laws based on many other instructions from God, but this one just didn't make the cut. In my mind, there are two reasons why it didn't. Reason number one is that people like to get drunk. Reason number two is that there is too much money to be made to allow such a law to be enforced.

From a manufacturer's standpoint, I can understand this. No one wants to tell their target consumers to go easy on the amount of money spent on their products. To be fair, companies who produce alcoholic beverages do urge their consumers to drink responsibly. The irony here is that this responsibility falls upon the heads of the consumers whose ability to act responsibly becomes impaired after consuming those companies' products. This is just my observation. I left freedom and rights out of the equation on purpose as they often serve as lids that seal off discussions about what's inside the jar. Yet another observation is that our responsibility concerning alcohol goes beyond not getting drunk.

If you've ever had to explain to someone that drinking alcohol is not a sin, you were likely defending your position against someone who felt that your drinking in any capacity conflicted with your Christian faith. Unless you were speaking from a podium when you did this, you likely set only one person straight. If other acquaintances with similar perceptions toward alcohol were present, they may have chosen to remain silent and harbor their reproach until a little later when they could tell someone else about your drinking. You wouldn't be present to defend yourself this time. Thankfully, there is a strategy that will eliminate this type of fallout. Now addressing the Romans, Paul adds insight to the messages he delivered to the Ephesians and the Philippians.

Do not destroy the work of God for the sake of food. All food is clean, but it is wrong for a man to eat anything that causes someone else to stumble. It is better not to eat meat or drink wine or to do anything else that will cause your brother to fall. So whatever you believe about these things keep between yourself and God. Blessed is the man who does not condemn himself by what he approves.

Romans 14:20-22

In this example, both food and drink are called "clean." On a dinner plate or in a drinking glass, these items are not harmful. However, among these clean and harmless consumables exists a variety that is often *believed* to be unclean or harmful. Eating meat isn't so much an issue today as it was back then (hallelujah!), but alcohol still fuels many fires among the hard stances in favor of and against consuming it. Paul was well aware of this and taught us that followers of Jesus can avoid getting burned by not having our names associated with drinking alcohol. Not only can consuming it damage our testimonies, but also speaking out in favor of it.

As you may have concluded on your own, this is not a well-received strategy. In fact, a common response to this teaching goes something like, "It's not my problem if someone thinks I'm sinning when I'm not." To this, I would have to agree. It may not be that person's problem. Rather, it could be their *condemnation* as you just read. This applies when one knows the risk of leading others astray and proceeds to ignore God's will in favor of their own. I sense a fire starting among you. I'd hate for your new book to get scorched, so I will clarify that the Bible does not tell us that we cannot enjoy wine or beer. It does, however, instruct each of us to share the message of the gospel with others. And so we must question our ability to lead people to Christ while drinking. If you agree that wine or beer would put a damper on things, then you must determine whether taking yourself out of the game of soul-winning for any length of time in favor of alcohol is "making the most of every opportunity."

Regardless of our feelings toward alcohol consumption, there's no denying its potential to cause others to stumble. This is not a one-of-a-kind situation either. There are tons of activities that can send people around us the wrong message. And when salvation is at stake, we fare better by not taking part in *any* of them if there's even a small chance that doing so can send people running in the opposite direction of Jesus.

As tools for achieving God's will on earth, we must protect our soul-winning creds at all costs; never forgetting that the days are evil and the generation is crooked and perverse. Each of us who have made a public display of affection for our Savior can expect to be judged by the mere sight of our actions. It would be great if all people would look beyond the surface before passing judgment, but that requires an effort that many humans are unwilling to make. As a writer, being aware of this notion is extremely important. I'll explain why.

When you and I are out shopping for books, we read the summaries on the back covers of the ones we've judged by their front covers. Yes, I know. We're told never to do this. But it's how I, and likely you as well, shop for books. We reach for attractive covers whose titles reflect the topic or genre we'd like to read, and then hope the summaries on the back are just as captivating. A writer must be very selective over the wording in his or her book's summary or *back cover copy* as it is more commonly called. If the summary is too lengthy, the book will be returned to the shelf. That may sound like odd behavior from people who enjoy reading for hours at a time, but it happens often enough to warrant this strategy. The summary must also be an accurate representation of a book's content. A book whose cover tells of a modern murder mystery and whose pages tell of a young girl's love for churning butter in the 1930's is not going to fly. The author of this book will have a tough time selling a new one.

The goal is to grab readers' attention with a book's cover and leave them wanting to read the much larger version of the summary on the pages beneath it. I believe we can all agree that there's no fair comparison between an entertaining book and a person's character. Each of their values is vastly different from the other. Even so, it takes little more than an undesirable cover for the messages each one delivers to be completely dismissed. As followers of Christ, our lives are associated with the Bible. You might even say we serve as book covers for God's Word. The task we are given, however, is not limited to delivering its content but accurately *reflecting* its content in all that we do. And, unlike stories on the best-seller list that can be skipped over with no real consequences, the content we have to share is vital to the lives of every living soul on earth.

As for our lesson, I have chosen Paul's "better" by not drinking alcoholic beverages at all. It only took reading through those verses once to make my decision. I simply could not fathom risking my ability be a credible witness for Christ. This surrender went far beyond alcohol too. My will had been taking precedence over God's in numerous areas of my life. While I've made some great progress toward a reversal, I anticipate this being a struggle that I'll deal with for the rest of my life.

Regarding our teacher, Paul shares the title, *Apostle* with Jesus' disciples. This title distinguished these men as ministers who received Jesus' teachings first-hand. Paul, however, was not around during Jesus' ministry and was not named among the twelve disciples. It was after the resurrection that Paul was commissioned personally by the risen Christ. If you already understand this, then great. There are some who may not, so I thought I'd put it out there. No, I'm not sure what Paul's last name was. Thanks for asking though!

It is November of 2017 as I write this last portion of the chapter. I'm well into the editing phase of the book, so you could say that I'm writing to you from the future that has already passed. There have been many corrections and sentence restructures, but I've not added any significant content until now. My encounter with a superhero simply had to be included.

Today is the day that the film, *Wonder Woman* was released into theaters worldwide. Playing the starring role is Gal Gadot, an actress whose catchy name I'd never heard before. My daughter had been itching to see the movie, so I decided to Google a few reviews. While there were indeed critics' reviews in my search results, they suffered in comparison to the number of articles criticizing one of the actress's body parts. Apparently, Gal's performance revealed that her underarms missed the tanning treatment that the rest of her got. Such cruelty was being expressed in these articles over such a trivial matter. This behavior is nothing new, of course. But I still managed to feel somewhat astonished by it. I felt that the attitudes behind what I was reading were like animals lurking in the darkness, waiting for the slightest chance to pounce on their prey. Then it hit me. I'd read this very analogy before.

Be alert and of sober mind. Your enemy the devil prowls around like a roaring lion looking for someone to devour.

1 Peter 5:8

Be careful out there.

13 A Testimony

You probably noticed that I did not include an introduction at the beginning of this book. I always intended to put one there. But I figure whichever chapter number this one ends up with is as good a place as any. Readers do like to know a bit about the authors they are reading, especially Christian authors who have compelling testimonies to share. I do have one, rest assured. But who I was prior to attaining my identity in Christ is not part of it. I'll tell you why before I begin.

Throughout my years, I listened to a great number of personal testimonies. Each was delivered in front of either my Sunday school class or the congregation at church and featured a unique story about what life was like prior to becoming saved. Although the stories were interesting, and while I was certainly glad to hear of the many decisions to follow Jesus, the uplifting feeling one hopes to receive from these victorious reports never entered me. Rather, I felt a bit down over my own testimony. It wasn't filled with the horrific drama that sparked sighs of sympathy and shouts of "Amen" from among the congregation. In my mind, it had no place among these moving speeches. So, I never shared it.

Today, I can admit that I was wrong in my reluctance to share my testimony. Sure, my life story wouldn't sell out a theater with only four seats. But that's just it. My testimony shouldn't be about me. It's God's work that sells tickets. When it comes to salvation, each of us arrived on the same boat. So, our testimonies shouldn't be focused on how bad the waves rocked us. You've likely heard one of these where the spotlight on one's sins is followed by a celebration of that person's freedom from their old ways. God is given credit, of course, but the story ends just before they exit the boat.

I also learned that there is no varying degree of being lost. The man who comes to Christ after removing a loaded pistol from his temple experiences no greater transition to salvation than the man who simply picks up his Bible and starts reading. In the ninth chapter of the book of John, we read what must be the shortest and yet the most memorable testimony throughout the ages. Mine's a little longer.

. . . I was blind, but now I see!
John 9:25

A TESTIMONY

Being raised in a Christian family, I cannot recall a time when I didn't know who God was. I knew about Jesus' sacrifice and of the many stories surrounding his death and resurrection, but it took me sixteen years to finally want to become saved. Even so, the new person I was to become after being raised from the water during my baptism never really surfaced. I was the same kid; just wet. No one at the church I was attending at that time ever told me what I should do next, so I just went about life the way I saw fit. Aside from my occasional guilty prayer, I had no real interaction with God. I read the Bible, but my motivation was nothing more than the accomplishment of having read it in a year. I didn't know there was a thing called *knowing God* that I was to be striving for, so I didn't reach out to Him. He, however, reached out to me.

I was in my early twenties when I first encountered God moving in my life. It was quite startling to experience something from within that I had no control over; something so different, so incredible. My heart was being transformed by a very specific message God was delivering. And I quickly wrote it down. As excited as I was over this message, I wasn't sure what to do with it. So, the excitement I was feeling soon left. Months later, I received God's message again. This time, I grabbed a pen and wrote several pages, not knowing exactly why. I had never written anything beyond what I was instructed to write in school, and I certainly don't recall being any good at it. But somehow it was the natural response. What did God say in His message? He said, "My children are not listening to Me."

He delivered this message over and over during the years that followed. And each instance resulted in pages of written text. It was when God's message changed that I finally gave my heart over to Him completely. The new message was piercing and consisted of only three words. "You aren't either." I was blindsided by my own blindness.

Today I am no longer blind, but see just as the man did who was given sight at the touch of Jesus. What do I see exactly? I see God. I see God providing me a new heart that desires Him above all things. I see God moving me to use abilities I never knew I had to serve Him. I see God providing me with opportunities to share the love I have for Him with others. I see God entrusting me with His word that I have come to cherish. I see God molding my children into sponges for His teaching. I see God drawing my wife and me closer to each other and to Him as we raise them together. I see God. And I see Him working in my life every day. My written responses to God's messages continue. I pray that you might also see God working in your own life as you read each of them in this book.

14 Excessive Perfection

The word, *excessive* means to go beyond the proper limit. I know because I checked. While the word has no negative connotations, it is most commonly used to express negativity. For instance, a woman who is told she's going overboard—beyond the proper limit, was likely doing something to an extent that became displeasing to the person who made the comment. If it was her rambling that was called excessive, she was probably rambling to the point of annoying that person who may not have been annoyed had she rambled a lesser amount. I fear that I may be approaching this point myself so I'll move on.

In this chapter, I do feel an analysis of what people call excessive is warranted in order to present this topic in the clearest way possible. Let's begin by examining a simple question. Can our love for God be excessive? Put another way, can we love God too much? Since there's no line I know of that we should be wary of exceeding, I think it's safe to conclude that we cannot. In fact, I'm certain that none of us can love God the way Jesus commands us to. Does this make Jesus' expectations excessive? Absolutely not. Confused yet? Don't worry. I'm getting there.

When it comes to sin, Jesus will condone none of it. He will never tell us it's ok to sin even once. He demonstrated this in the Bible when he commanded those he encountered not to sin again and to go without sin. And yet there is zero chance that any of them actually did. They probably didn't even make it until dinner before tripping up. Living a sinless life is not possible for humans. Jesus knew this about us. He knew we couldn't be any other way. This is why he succumbed to God's will and gave himself over to be crucified. So, why would Jesus tell us to be perfect if he knows we can't be? It's because he *deserves* nothing less than our perfection. And God deserves to be loved perfectly. And so, instead of being excessive or unreasonable, these expectations are appropriate, sufficient, and just. My trusty thesaurus will back me up here.

Jesus set the bar of his expectations above our reach so that we would do the same. It's when we see God's expectations as excessive that our hearts settle for less than the perfection He deserves. Our salvation is all about what we can't do instead of what we can. One of the things we cannot do is *be good*. Why? It's because God's definition of *good* is perfection. To Him, a thing cannot be called good even if it's only one percent not good. This places us among the things that are not good.

God tells us plainly that, left to ourselves, we can do nothing good. And yet, God does call attention to goodness that we can possess. This goodness is called faith. So, how can people who can do no good come to have this faith? God gives it to us. Not only is God the provider of faith, but also the transformer of hearts. And He chose whose hearts He would transform before the earth was created. To those He chose, salvation would be given.

For those whom He foreknew, He also predestined to become conformed to the image of His Son, so that He would be the firstborn among many brethren; and these whom He predestined, He also called; and these whom He called, He also justified; and these whom He justified, He also glorified.

Romans 8:29-30

As you just read, our being saved has nothing to do with our own efforts. We often call salvation a decision, but it's clear that a person can't just decide to do good if they are incapable of good. Instead, God, who is indeed good, moves us to salvation. He foreknows, He predestines, He calls, He justifies, and He glorifies. God literally does it all. So, how does free will play into all this? Free will is all we do that is *not* good. Since God can do nothing bad, we're left holding the bag. So, while salvation is all God's doing, our sin nature is evidence that we are not programmed like robots.

Coming to terms with this reality isn't easy. I wrestled with the idea of God selecting some but not others for quite a while. I remember thinking, "How on earth can this be fair?" God eventually answered this question for me. *On earth*, it cannot be fair.

"For My thoughts are not your thoughts, nor are your ways My ways," declares the Lord.

Isaiah 55:8

Concerning fairness, this next verse helped me to understand that no one gets a door slammed in their face when it comes to salvation. If a man or woman wants to know God, they will not be denied.

For everyone who asks receives; the one who seeks finds; and to the one who knocks, the door will be opened.

Matthew 7:8

Stubbornness presented yet another hurdle in my ability to come to terms with this truth. I had become so insistent that becoming saved was my own decision that I created an image of God that was not of His likeness. In this image, I supposed God simply knew all the choices we would make up front and saved each of us accordingly. This is actually a popular view of how God works. Unfortunately, it limits His power to that of a psychic. He doesn't just know all and see all. He orchestrates salvation because we're incapable of doing anything to achieve it on our own. We are saved according to God's plan. How wonderful it is to know that you and I are part of it.

Trusting in God over our own understanding goes against our human nature to battle uncertainty and demand explanations. We can challenge God's omniscience with our own reasoning until we're blue in the face, but resistance to the truth is futile. Submission to it, on the other hand, is life-changing. If right now you're thinking we should just throw up our hands and surrender our hearts and minds to God, I'm with you one hundred percent. Let's all do that together.

15 First Love

With so many instructions to adhere to within the Bible, it's easy to allow the motivation behind our obedience to shift from one factor to another. We've just determined that our works bear no weight in our salvation. And yet there is much we are expected to do as Christians. All of Jesus' calls to action are in our best interest. They protect us and teach us how to channel the love that develops within our hearts for God. An effort to return thanks, however, can become something else without our intention or knowledge that it's happening. An awakening that reveals just how far we've gone off course can be very scary indeed.

A few months ago, my family began the two-hour drive to my wife's parents' home to celebrate my father-in-law's birthday. After driving an hour, we made a rest stop to accommodate the two small bladders in our back seat. Heading back to the freeway with the open country as far as the eye can see in both directions, I proceeded to the entrance ramp leading back toward our home. It wasn't until "How much further, Daddy?" that I began to question the accuracy of Google Maps. I had driven for an hour and forty minutes, yet we were still an hour and forty minutes from our destination. Oh, the scorn that I and others in the car piled upon my absent-mindedness when we realized I had gone the wrong way! As much as I wanted to share the blame with those I felt should equally have been paying attention, only one brain was responsible. Let us now add some company to this misery with a story of a girl who experienced a similar awakening.

Meet Rhianne. Rhianne is in her early thirties and has a tremendous love for flowers. Rather than a gardener, she considers herself merely an enthusiast of all things floral. Secretly, she could do without getting her hands all grimy with soil and fertilizer, but she knows that it comes with the territory of having such a fondness for flowers. She shared this love with her favorite aunt who she spent a great deal of time with inside the greenhouse that her late uncle had built for his wife. Shortly before her own passing, Rhianne's aunt gave her a rare blue orchid that the two had dreamed of owning for years. Rhianne treasured its lovely flowers that they both agreed looked like the wings of an angel. And now, this special gift would be given constant attention in memory of the life she shared with her dearly departed aunt who she missed terribly.

One evening, Rhianne was enjoying a cup of coffee at the little shop she and her aunt frequented together when a girl about her age commented on the book she was reading. It had a large purple orchid on its cover and would be hard to miss by a fellow enthusiast which this girl indeed was. After a pleasant conversation, she invited Rhianne to join her and two friends who met each week to just hang out and talk about gardening. Rhianne was excited over the invitation and joined the group of ladies for their next gathering.

While she certainly enjoyed the company of her newfound friends, Rhianne often felt inferior to the level of knowledge each of them was sharing. "They were pros," she thought as they traded notes over the latest gardening tools and planting techniques. Each spoke of the wide array of flowers they maintained, whereas Rhianne's efforts had become focused on a single orchid. They watched shows and subscribed to periodicals that Rhianne had no knowledge of, and bonded over sharing opinions that she did not possess. Needless to say, Rhianne felt out of place. "This is going to change," she thought as she took notes of all the things they had that she didn't.

By their fifth meeting together, Rhianne was able to talk about all the new tools she had purchased and share her thoughts on the articles and shows the other girls had been enjoying. She also shared with them the selection of flowers she chose for her new garden that covered a large area near her dainty backyard shed.

Rhianne had become exhausted over all the new activities she took on, but felt they were worthwhile as her inclusion within this special group of friends became more substantiated. Meanwhile, her treasured orchid became increasingly neglected. She must have walked by it twenty times before realizing its petals had all fallen off, leaving a withered stem in her aunt's ornate planter.

Back in Chapter 2, we learned of the letters that Jesus dictated to his then elderly disciple, John during a surprise visit. The letter we'll look at now is the one that was drafted for the church at Ephesus. To this church, Jesus offered praise for their hard work and for their intolerance for evil. Their job well done also included a propensity to call out and then throw out the traveling con men of that day who claimed to be apostles. The church members had become so focused on keeping out the bad elements that they neglected the precious element they were protecting.

**You have forsaken the love you had at first.
Consider how far you have fallen!
Repent and do the things you did at first . . .**

Revelation 2:4-5

With every new thing we learn, we make adjustments or corrections to our ways of thinking. Realizing we've been wrong about something can be a real bummer. But it isn't always earth-shattering the way it must have been at Ephesus. These little corrections are often quite wonderful. I'll let you in on one of my own.

Over the last year alone, I cannot count the times I missed my scheduled time with God. I would wake up in the morning intent on praying and enjoying coffee over God's Word, only to become sidetracked by emails, texts, kids who forgot their lunches, and other responsibilities. Whenever this would occur, guilt would seize my entire being. In my mind, I had stood God up and let Him down all in one sitting. So, I would ask His forgiveness for allowing these things to get in the way. The sympathetic head nods I detect among you let me know I'm not alone. I'd ask you to join me on my quest to determine why we're so bad at maintaining our lists of priorities, but I already found the culprit. It's our minds.

Whenever we use our hearts to devise a list of priorities, our minds secretly make their own conflicting list. Our hearts tell us what we want to do while our minds focus on what we need to do instead. This struggle between our hearts and minds occurs from the moment we wake until the wee hours of the morning when we fall asleep in our comfy chairs while trying to finish writing our books. That part may only apply to me, but I do have a universal solution concerning God's placement among our priorities. The solution? Remove God from your list.

Whaaaat??? If that was your reaction, you read that last sentence correctly. God has no desire to be ranked among our earthly activities. Our fitting Him into busy schedules that we maintain so poorly has to be equally undesirable to Him. So, go ahead and remove Him from your priorities. Now insert God into every remaining item on your list. Instead of God, family, work, hobbies, etc., your list should include God during your family activities, God amidst your work hours, and enjoying God in your leisure time, or "scheduled fun" as my wife likes to call it.

When we come to desire God above all else, our hearts make this adjustment automatically. It's our minds that make us feel we need to place a checkmark next to His name. I'm not saying we should never set aside time to be alone with God. On the contrary, we should all do this regularly. Just know that having an aching heart after missing that appointment is not a bad thing. Rather, it's a wonderful thing that we should rejoice over. It's how we know we're looking up and that our first love is still the object of our hearts' desires.

16 Sin & Treatment

As we go out into the world seeking those who have not yet have not yet trusted in Jesus, we will encounter every type of personality. Some we will gravitate toward while making a conscious effort to avoid others. Why would we avoid some of these people? We do it because of their sin. Our tendency to seek out good people and avoid known sinners is part of our human nature. This was not Jesus' nature though. Despite being fully human, his being fully God at the same time led Jesus to seek out those whose identities were synonymous with their sin.

Sin has existed in this world from the earliest days recorded in scripture. There will be no new sin in the future that the Bible hasn't already addressed. We know this because God exists in the beginning, in the end, and every day in between at all times. While you and I existed in the past and will exist in the future, God simply *is*. At no time is He *not*. God sees the entire picture always from a current perspective. And, because He does, we can be certain that His feelings toward sin do not change. Our feelings, however, tend to change with the tides. What was once without question can become questionable in our minds. When this occurs, we feel that God should lighten up on His sin policy to accommodate our new ways of thinking.

Homosexuality is one such sin that Christian attitudes differ greatly over. There will always be those on God's side of the argument. Many, however, have become sympathetic toward gay men and women. We have heard their defenses of being helpless against their homosexual desires and have begun to wonder if indeed they were "born that way" and given "no choice" in the matter. Believe it or not, both of these claims are accurate.

In the Bible, we are assured that every human who lives and breathes was born with a natural gravitation toward sin. And, as Scripture also teaches us, none of us were given a choice to opt out of our sinful natures. And so the argument for homosexuals being a group of people who got the short end of the stick is not a valid one. But this is what we are being led to believe. Christians who become swayed to this way of thinking simply add weight to their case for the right of their sin. This mindset also makes God into a cruel manipulator of the defenseless.

When Jesus gave his life as a sacrifice for the sins of the world, he did so without regard to specific sins or sinners. Sin is not specific to homosexual acts, nor is the need to be forgiven. The Bible assures us that *all* have sinned and that *all* are desperately in need of the forgiveness that Jesus' made available to us. And yet we become fooled into believing that forgiveness of these sins should not be necessary.

Do not be deceived: Neither the sexually immoral nor idolaters nor adulterers nor men who have sex with men nor thieves nor the greedy nor drunkards nor slanderers nor swindlers will inherit the kingdom of God.

1 Corinthians 6:9-10

In this passage, sinners are labeled according to the sin they practice. This verse alone may lead us to believe that these individuals are both helpless and hopeless. The verse that immediately follows, however, assures us that this is not the case.

And that is what some of you were. But you were washed, you were sanctified, you were justified in the name of the Lord Jesus Christ and by the Spirit of our God.

1 Corinthians 6:11

In this verse, the word, "were" is used four times. It informs us of those who no longer fit the profiles in the preceding verses. Each of them was given a new profile in Christ upon recognizing their sin and turning away from it. Could this transformation have occurred if those people believed that their sins did not need to be forgiven? Of course not. Their salvation was dependent upon the truth; truth delivered in a manner free of condescension and threatening words.

Have you ever reached into a birdcage to get a parakeet to perch on your finger? Your movement needs to be slow and gentle for the bird to trust in the safety of your hand. When the bird realizes you mean it no harm, it will be easier for it to hop onto your finger the next time. But if instead, you were to snap your fingers, the bird will flap its wings violently in order to get away from you. Gaining trust after an episode like that will be a chore if you can do it at all.

This is what has happened with many of our lost brothers and sisters. Instead of extending our hands in love, we've snapped our fingers and shaken our Bibles in judgment, leaving a trail of bitterness in our wake. While this behavior is not representative of a *genuine* Christian, those scorned in the name of Jesus couldn't care less. The baby can join the bath water as far as they're concerned. And who can blame them? I certainly wouldn't have anything to do with a business whose salesman tracked mud in my home.

Going back to the young rich man, when Jesus pointed out his fault, he did so out of love. Each time this story is told, we find no text that leads us to believe Jesus was spiteful in his approach. Instead, the picture painted in the books of Matthew, Mark, and Luke is of a gentle and loving Jesus who became sad as he watched the man sulk over his reluctant heart. Following Jesus' example, we should be relaying God's will in a loving manner and offering the assurance of forgiveness and salvation that Jesus made available to all of us.

In Chapter 12, we examined the term, *reproach*. Used similarly is the word, *rebuke* which refers to the process of pointing out sinful behavior with the intention of correcting those who are engaged in it. To some, a successful attempt at rebuking involves a poster board with "hell" written on it to emphasize as the consequence of the sin being picketed. The Bible, however, refers to the rebuking process the restoration of fellow Christians whose sin caused them to wander away as a sheep does from its shepherd.

Brothers and sisters, if someone is caught in a sin, you who live by the Spirit should restore that person gently. But watch yourselves, or you also may be tempted.

Galatians 6:1

When works of art are restored, meticulous measures are taken to return them to a state that reflects their original beauty. A careless conservator can cause a painting to become unfit to be put on display. If that ruined painting was a Rembrandt, the conservator might be reassigned to help restore the functionality of a guillotine in the artifact wing.

The restoration of a person whose behavior conflicts with God's will must also be done delicately. We are to usher that person back to being obedient with the same gentle demeanor that Jesus displayed. After all, we're all Rembrandts in the eyes of our wonderful creator. And there's no sin we can commit that makes us unfit for His affection.

17 Know Your Enemy

It's 5:15am. I'd been lying awake since 4:00 so I figured I'd make some coffee and begin my day. I'm glad to see all of you are still here. In a bit, you're going to some banging noises from upstairs. Don't be alarmed. It's just a grumpy pre-teen getting ready for school. If you followed me when I took out the trash a few minutes ago, you saw a beautiful fall morning with red and orange trees, glistening blades of grass, a hint of fog, and a soaking wet Amazon box that I totally missed yesterday. I'm not worried though. Pralines from Savannah, Georgia always come wrapped inside. That's not really what's in there. But it sounds much better than socks and boxers.

By now you've all learned that *looking up* is all about the positioning of our hearts rather than our eyes. Our eyes, however, will aid us tremendously as we pursue the closeness of our savior. Not only must we recognize by sight the many people who will guide us on the path of righteousness, but equally those who exist to make that path undetectable. These are our enemies whose weapons are distortions of the truth. And we are urged to prepare for a stand-off with each one of them.

Put on the whole armor of God, that you may be able to stand against the schemes of the devil.
Ephesians 6:11

Satan's schemes take many forms. They are present in churches, institutions, public teachings, and belief systems; all of which derive from the influence of Satan in the lives of human beings. Regardless of whether people mean to inflict harm, we can be certain that the one behind their attacks has an agenda to destroy God's church and stop His plan from playing out on this earth. This can't happen, of course. God's chosen cannot be stripped from His grasp, and the ending as it is written cannot be altered. So why would Satan fight this losing battle? It's because he believes he can win. He believed this when he was banished from heaven, and he believes it still today.

As followers of Christ, we must know that Satan is powerless against our salvation. He can, however, cause the confusion, turmoil, and anguish that many of us suffer through. And so we must be properly equipped to overcome his evil schemes and the temptations associated with them. But we first must be able to recognize evil. This may sound easy to do, but evil doesn't always appear evil. Sometimes it appears holy.

Beware of false prophets, who come to you in sheep's clothing but inwardly are ravenous wolves.

Matthew 7:15

Just before the solar eclipse that occurred in August of 2017, there was a flood of videos added to YouTube by people who claimed that God revealed to them His plans for Christ's return. While some relied on charts and graphs with hidden codes that the Bible reportedly revealed, the majority of these claimed that God had spoken to them in their dreams. These "oracles" appear every time the weather changes it seems. And yet the church remains on the earth after each signal. You and I may not be quick to call these YouTuber prophets our enemies, but God is.

Behold, I am against those who have prophesied false dreams," declares the Lord, "and related them and led My people astray

by their falsehoods and reckless boasting; yet I did not send them or command them, nor do they furnish this people the slightest benefit," declares the Lord.

Then as for the prophet or the priest or the people who say, 'The oracle of the Lord,' I will bring punishment upon that man and his household.

For you will no longer remember the oracle of the Lord, because every man's own word will become the oracle, and you have perverted the words of the living God, the Lord of hosts, our God.

Jeremiah 23:32, 34, 36

I never went back and checked to see if these videos were still there after the eclipse. I just assumed that they were taken down. I mean, who wants to leave a trail of debunked claims about God? Well, apparently many churches do. And they're standing by their reports that God desires wealth and prosperity for His children instead of the suffering that Jesus told us about. Some churches associated with the Christian faith have even begun to embrace sin in the manner we discussed in the previous chapter. Instead of being increasingly separate from a world growing more wicked, many of our churches are taking strides to blend in. This is called *evolving* according to what I've read. And with each new evolution, there's a group of people who will jump at the opportunity to be a part of it. After all, who wants suffering and conviction? Right?

For the time will come when people will not put up with sound doctrine. Instead, to suit their own desires, they will gather around them a great number of teachers to say what their itching ears want to hear.

2 Timothy 4:3

Our enemies aren't just coming up with new deviations from scripture. Many are holding on to the deviations that have been around for ages. In your neighborhood, there is a church that embraces man-made doctrine under the impression that Jesus' blood was not sufficient to cover our sins. And so it set up a system of hoops that the congregation must jump through, lest they lose their salvation. This same church insists that its members refrain from reading the Bible and that its administration must interpret it for them. At this, you have to think that there's a portion of the Bible not being interpreted correctly if it's being interpreted at all.

If you recognize this church as your own, God has a message for you.

Come out of her, my people, so that you will not share in her sins

Revelation 18:4

God makes it very clear how we are to regard, read, and use Scripture. When His instructions are followed correctly, we may use His truth to discern, discredit, and conquer. There is, however, a purpose for knowing our enemies that outweighs any victory we can claim. It is so our hearts can become broken for them.

You have heard that it was said, 'Love your neighbor and hate your enemy.' But I tell you, love your enemies and pray for those who persecute you...

Matthew 5:43-44

God wants to know your enemy. Pray that God can use you to lead a misguided adversary to Jesus.

18 Predictive Text

When we hear the word, *prophecy*, a feeling of uneasiness comes over us. This is because we associate the term with all things dark and mysterious. In everything from conspiracy theories to Christopher Walken movies, the topic has been used to add ominous tones to creative content. In Scripture, prophecies are messages about future events that were delivered by God to be spoken aloud by the people of His choosing. These messengers of prophecy were called prophets. While many of these messages served as warnings about imminent consequences for disobedience to God, not all were gloom and doom. In fact, Jesus' birth, death, and resurrection were all prophesied. Jesus himself also spoke of many future events. He wasn't a prophet though. He was God. And he still is.

The reason I've chosen to dive into this topic has to do the verse that inspired this book's title. It's been a while since we read it together, so I'll paste it in once again. The two words we'll be examining now are "these things." When Jesus spoke these words, he had just finished delivering a speech filled with scary details about events that will take place during the earth's final years. I will attempt to paint this picture for you.

Now when these things begin to happen, look up and lift your heads, because your redemption draws near.

Luke 21:28

In the city of Jerusalem, thirteen men were walking together and enjoying each other's company. They had just entered the streets of the city after a visit to the Jewish temple when one of the men made a remark about the temple's beauty. Expecting a response that complimented his observation, the man was met with a reply of a different sort. None of them were prepared for what was said.

Jesus, who was leading this family of men, caught each of them off guard when he told them that the temple would one day be totally destroyed. Jesus spoke about the future often, causing an air of perplexity among the men. This time they were not going to let him off easy. After a short discussion among themselves, the disciples decided to ask Jesus about the future event each of them agreed was the most important—the day that Jesus would be coming back. This wasn't the first time the men grilled Jesus for information. They knew he was leaving but had no clue how or why. His answers just didn't make sense to them. Even so, Jesus' presence took priority over his absence on this day. So, to oblige their anxious hearts, Jesus gave his disciples an earful of prophecies about events that would signal his return.

You will be hearing of wars and rumors of wars. See that you are not frightened, for those things must take place, but that is not yet the end. Nation will rise against nation, and kingdom against kingdom. There will be famines and earthquakes in various places. All these are the beginning of birth pains.

Matthew 24:6-8

For then there will be a great tribulation, such as has not occurred since the beginning of the world until now, nor ever will. Unless those days had been cut short, no life would have been saved; but for the sake of the elect those days will be cut short.

Matthew 24:21-22

In a world where "rumors" can be shot down in a matter of minutes over social media, you've got to think that his use of the word meant something else. And it did. Jesus was describing *threats* of war that would be significant at that time. His speech also warned the men about the many false prophets who would come out of the woodwork, a surge of wickedness in the world, and the likelihood of their deaths by execution. All the world would hate them according to Jesus. With the disciples' mouths likely hanging wide open in astonishment, Jesus ended the speech with a tremendous emphasis on their need to be ready.

Therefore keep watch, because you do not know on what day your Lord will come. But understand this: If the owner of the house had known at what time of night the thief was coming, he would have kept watch and would not have let his house be broken into. So you also must be ready, because the Son of Man will come at an hour when you do not expect him.

Matthew 24:42-44

There are many who feel that these prophecies are too vague to prompt an immediate response. I will certainly agree that wars and earthquakes are nothing new. And we've seen efforts to end famine on TV for years. So why should these events make us want to jumpstart a Bible study? The events shouldn't. Jesus should.

Jesus replied to them, "When it is evening, you say, 'It will be fair weather, for the sky is red.' And in the morning, 'There will be a storm today, for the sky is red and threatening.' Do you know how to discern the appearance of the sky, but cannot discern the signs of the times?

Matthew 16:2-3

Jesus said this to the Pharisees when they did not recognize the one sign that signaled the coming of the Messiah. That sign was standing right in front of them. And there are indeed signs that have appeared before our own eyes as well. In the next chapter, we'll take a look at some very specific events foretold in the Bible that have occurred in recent years. If you weren't looking up, however, you likely missed them.

19 Signs & Signals

My goal for this chapter is to share with you what God has revealed to me concerning biblical prophecy. He has revealed each of these events to you as well and has urged each of us to recognize them when they occur. Of all the chapters in this book, this one stands to receive the most scrutiny. I've even been advised not to include this information due to the high likelihood of being wrong in my pairing of current events with those foretold in the Bible. That advice was duly noted and appreciated.

Keep in mind that I am not putting words in God's mouth the way the way the individuals we spoke of earlier were doing in their videos on YouTube. Each of these events are already described in our Bible. I am simply pointing out what God tells us we will see if we look up. And it is well with my soul to share this with you. This will be the longest and, hopefully, the most exciting chapter we'll go over together. I pray that its impact on you mirrors

LOOKING UP: LIVING IN ANTICIPATION OF CHRIST

the tremendous effect it's had on me and my relationship with God. Oh! I almost forgot. Before we get started, my wife wanted me to ask if any of you would like a smoothie. She puts leaves in them. No? Ok. Please tell her I asked if she mentions it. Everyone ready? Let's begin.

The following events were prophesied to occur in the latter days; each one foretold before the birth of our Lord, Jesus Christ. I highly recommend having your internet browser available to corroborate them.

In the 17th chapter of his book, the prophet, Isaiah reveals what God would have us to know about the future of Damascus, Syria.

See, Damascus will no longer be a city but will become a heap of ruins.

In that day their strong cities, which they left because of the Israelites, will be like places abandoned to thickets and undergrowth. And all will be desolation.

Isaiah 17:1,9

In these verses, not only are we told of Damascus' imminent demise, but also of the party responsible for its destruction. If you're into world history, you likely know that Damascus has been deemed the oldest continually inhabited city in the world. Today, whichever city is second in line for this title has great potential to steal this record as Damascus, Syria was destroyed by Israel in 2013. The city's remains are not completely desolate though. Its war-torn structures and crumbled buildings serve as torture chambers and starvation camps for terrorist regimes. Needless to say, there is no welcome wagon for returning residents who heeded Israel's warning to evacuate. And, per Isaiah, we can expect the city to remain in this broken and abandoned state.

Take a moment to do a Google image search for the current state of Damascus. You'll get the picture—literally. There are many who will challenge this biblical correlation with the claim that Damascus was destroyed much earlier; in 732BC to be exact. While the city was indeed captured in this period of history, we do know that its state of being inhabited continued on to become renowned in the 21st century.

God continues to use Isaiah to warn of judgment coming to the Egyptians. In chapter 19, the prophet speaks about a time in the latter days when a merciless ruler would come into power over Egypt, resulting in a civil war among the Egyptian people.

"I will stir up Egyptian against Egyptian— brother will fight against brother, neighbor against neighbor, city against city, kingdom against kingdom."

Isaiah 19:2

"I will hand the Egyptians over to the power of a cruel master, and a fierce king will rule over them," declares the Lord, the Lord Almighty.

Isaiah 19:4

The year 2012 saw Egypt's first and only democratically elected president, Mohamed Morsi, who turned his back on the values he touted to the Egyptian people during his campaign. Once elected, Morsi granted himself absolute power that allowed his Muslim Brotherhood to rewrite the Egyptian constitution according to Islamic law. When this occurred, a deadly civil war broke out between Egyptians who supported Morsi and those who opposed him.

If you watched this event unfold on the news, you might recall segments that were shown to inform the world of Egypt's environmental and economic conditions. The news correspondent I watched might as well have been reading directly from the Bible.

The waters of the river will dry up, and the riverbed will be parched and dry. The canals will stink; the streams of Egypt will dwindle and dry up. The reeds and rushes will wither, also the plants along the Nile, at the mouth of the river. Every sown field along the Nile will become parched, will blow away and be no more. The fishermen will groan and lament, all who cast hooks into the Nile; those who throw nets on the water will pine away. Those who work with combed flax will despair, the weavers of fine linen will lose hope. The workers in cloth will be dejected, and all the wage earners will be sick at heart.

Isaiah 19:5-10

At this time, I invite you to set this book aside, or simply switch apps if you're reading on a device, and search YouTube for "Nile River drying." Choose one of the videos whose thumbnail image shows a heap of trash. These trash dumps were once underwater, but have become exposed as the canals that stretch off of the Nile's main waterway become dry. The stench is appropriately described, as is the crumbling fishing industry. The exporting of fine linens has also taken a hit as a result of the Nile's steadily diminishing water levels.

Each aspect of God's judgment is present in this news story that aired in 2010. Well, there was one that wasn't mentioned, but only because it hadn't happened yet.

The Lord will strike Egypt with a plague; he will strike them and heal them. They will turn to the Lord, and he will respond to their pleas and heal them.

Isaiah 19:22

In the year 2013, a swarm of locusts, unprecedented in size, arrived and began to ravage Southern Egypt, which is where 90% of the population resides. The swarms of these fist-size locusts darkened the skies in some areas and blanketed the ground with eggs that rapidly produced even more. YouTube also has this event captured by Egyptian locals who reference the book of Exodus to describe the size of the swarm. Ironically, these locusts appeared just before the Passover Festival in Israel.

Let's now hear from the prophet, Ezekiel regarding a war that many of us know as Armageddon. This war will occur in the future. But we can already see God's preparations for it.

You will come from your place in the far north, you and many nations with you, all of them riding on horses, a great horde, a mighty army. You will advance against my people Israel like a cloud that covers the land. In days to come, Gog, I will bring you against my land, so that the nations may know me when I am proved holy through you before their eyes.

Ezekiel 38:15-16

In chapter 38 of Ezekiel, we are told who the players will be in this monstrous attack on Israel. They include armies from the Persian nations of Iran, Afghanistan, Iraq, and Turkey, along with Southern Egypt, then referred to as Ethiopia. Leading this attack is Gog, which corresponds to the geographical location of Russia.

Ships will come from the shores of Cyprus; they will subdue Ashur and Eber, but they too will come to ruin.

Numbers 24:24

In this passage from the book of Numbers, the prophet, Balaam speaks of the Armageddon war against Ashur and Eber, who represent the descendants of the Hebrews, or Israel. In August of 2013, Russian warships assumed a permanent position in the Mediterranean Sea in order to maintain their own flavor of peace in the Middle East. And it was Syria that provided these ships with a docking port for fuel and supplies. When conflict within Syria depleted its resources, the Russian military was forced to dock elsewhere.

In February of 2015, the Russian docking port was moved to Cyprus, an island coastal to Israel where the seagoing Russian military replenishes its needs to this day.

Since God is orchestrating all of this unbeknownst to the orchestra, you may be wondering what motives exist among these nations to destroy Israel. Aside from the hatred that is God-fueled, there actually is something physical that He strategically placed to dangle in front of their faces.

. . . you will say, 'I will go up against the land of unwalled villages. I will go against those who are at rest, that live securely, all of them living without walls and having no

bars or gates, to capture spoil and to seize plunder . . .
Ezekiel 38:11-12

In 2009, one of the world's largest natural gas fields was discovered, conveniently tucked away beneath Israeli soil. And then they found another one, and then another and another. These discoveries have made Israel a major player in the exporting of energy. Surrounded by nations who are less than financially sound, the Holy Land has become a huge target. As the leader of this future band of thieves, Russia's crumbling economy puts them in a position to salivate over Israel's newfound prosperity. As for the absence of walls, the Bible assures us that the ones surrounding Jerusalem will come down after a peace treaty puts Israel's tensions at ease. It is during this period that a vulnerable Israel becomes surrounded by plunderers. And plunder they will until a certain king arrives to fight them off. This will be no ordinary king.

From His mouth comes a sharp sword, so that with it He may strike down the nations, and He will rule them with a rod of iron; and He treads the wine press of the fierce wrath of God, the Almighty. And on

His robe and on His thigh He has a name written, "KING OF KINGS, AND LORD OF LORDS."

Revelation 19:15-26

As tough as it is to imagine that the same prophets who foretold the birth of Jesus also spoke of events that would occur in the twenty-teens, the "proof is in the pudding" as they say. I'm not sure what kind of proof can be found in pudding, but I do know that the Bible does indeed prove itself over and over again to be the perfect and infallible word of God. If scripture advises something will occur, you can be certain that the event had either occurred already or will occur at some point in the future. And, as each one does occur, my excitement over our fast approaching day of redemption rises to new peaks.

I can't imagine anyone, Christian or non-believing, walking away unfazed after realizing they have witnessed God's work as foretold in the Bible. Sadly, I've no need to try to imagine this. I've seen with my own eyes those who refuse to acknowledge what God is calling to our attention to so that we might live our lives in a state of looking up. Non-Christians did not want to face the reality of the *existence* of God, while Christians did not want to face the reality of the *nearness* of God. Both believed that denial is but a river in Egypt. My friends, that river is running dry.

But if that evil slave says in his heart, 'My master is not coming for a long time,' and begins to beat his fellow slaves and eat and drink with drunkards; the master of that slave will come on a day when he does not expect *him* and at an hour which he does not know, and will cut him in pieces and assign him a place with the hypocrites; in that place there will be weeping and gnashing of teeth.

Matthew 24:48-51

20 Found Worthy

So, what do we do with all of this knowledge? Do we sell our homes, quit our jobs, and go sit in waiting out in the middle of a field somewhere? Absolutely not. There is still much work to be done—souls who need saving. Plotting dates and timelines in an attempt to pinpoint the end can be of no benefit either. As informative as the Bible is with events and time periods, Jesus assures us that no one can know when our big exit will occur.

> **But of that day or hour no one knows, not even the angels in heaven, nor the Son, but the Father alone.**
>
> Mark 13:32

As you can see, not even Jesus' calendar has the rapture date penciled in. And yet there had to be a reason he would get his disciples all riled up about his return. Thankfully there was a reason. That reason was, and still is, Jesus. He is the reason we are to live our lives looking up. He is the lover of our souls; the groom anxiously awaiting the arrival of his bride.

Let us rejoice and be glad and give the glory to Him, for the marriage of the Lamb has come and His bride has made herself ready.
Revelation 19:7

If you are a husband and felt it necessary to ask the father of your bride-to-be for his approval, stand up and tell us all about your experience. For those out of earshot, a reader from Florida described nervousness that prompted him to drink four cups of lukewarm coffee before he got up the confidence to ask. While coffee was likely a poor choice for calming the nerves, we can detect his anxiety over the situation. At that moment, there was nothing more important to him than being found worthy of marrying this man's daughter.

Imagine yourself standing before God with the same intentions for the granter of your salvation. The tables have now turned. You are no longer being judged for your worthiness of your bride's life, but of your bride's death. Here are some questions you'll want to be prepared to answer as you contend for your being found worthy.

- ❖ Do others know you for your love of God or for your earthly desires?

- ❖ Do you merely *profess* your faith or do you truly *possess* it?

- ❖ Do you seek God's will earnestly or have you no desire to read the Bible?

- ❖ Do you long for God's presence or is there no intimacy between you and Him?

As we come to a close, I urge you to reflect upon your own answers to these questions and the many others we've pondered together. While our answers will indeed be known to God when we are brought before His throne, you can be certain that they are known to Him at this very moment. My prayer for you upon completing this book is that you, in turn, would spend time with God in prayer over your life. Your heart may already be in the process of being transformed, but you can ask Him to help you attain the burning desire for Him that He wants for your heart. You can even rededicate your whole life to the service of one who gave up His own on your behalf.

And you can ask for opportunities to share this incredible love by naming God as the reason for the drastic change others see in you.

I recall a time when my young son was itching to join his friends from school for an online game on his PlayStation. When his mother made cleaning his room a condition before he could play, my son ran into his room and began to stir up dust with his speedy hands as he cleaned. After a little while, I realized he had not come out of his room. His allotted play time was nearly over, so I decided to check on him. As I approached his door expecting to hear books being slammed into place and his fast-moving feet on the floor, I was surprised to find total silence. As I moved my eye close to the small crack he left in the doorway, I saw that he was scribbling away on a piece of construction paper. I decided not to interrupt him, but finally did when it was time for him to get ready for bed. When he emerged from his room, he was carrying a beautiful likeness of him and his mother hand-in-hand that he had drawn for her. My son was only six at the time, so his artistic abilities were in their early stages. But his creation was perfect. That evening, there was no desire in his little heart that was any match for the love he had for his "mama."

There will be a day when God looks in on us with the intention of bringing us home. On that day, He wants to find us in the midst of our obedience out of an overwhelming love for Him. It is this magnitude of gratitude that makes us worthy of His son and grants us entry into our Father's Kingdom. As the day of our redemption draws near, let us prepare our hearts and be ready so that we will not be caught off guard. Instead, may we be found looking up, living in anticipation of Christ.

www.ingramcontent.com/pod-product-compliance
Lightning Source LLC
Chambersburg PA
CBHW031358040426
42444CB00005B/339